Odes of
Hafiz
Poetical Horoscope

Translated from the Persian by
Abbas Aryanpur Kashani, LL.D.

With an Introduction by
Manoochehr Aryanpur Kashani

MAZDA PUBLISHERS, Inc. ◆ Costa Mesa, California ◆
2004

Mazda Publishers, Inc.
Academic Publishers Since 1980
P.O. Box 2603
Costa Mesa, California 92628 U.S.A.
www.mazdapub.com

Library of Congress Cataloging Card Noumber: 84-61304
ISBN: 0-939214-253
ISBN 13: 978-0939214259
(alk. paper)

For my dear and loyal wife

INTRODUCTION

Shams-Oddin Mohammad Hafiz is the greatest and the most popular poet, especially of odes, in the Persian language. Even during his lifetime his fame had gone beyond his native land that he was known by the Tartar Tamerlane and revered by the Indian king of the Deccan. For over five centuries, Hafiz has remained the best known ode writer in the Persian-speaking world. His fame in the West, however, began in the last decade of the seventeenth century when Thomas Hyde published a Latin translation of the odes. In 1771, Count C. E. de Reviczki published a Latin translation of sixty odes. At about the same time, Sir William Jones (1746-94) began to publish his numerous English, French, Latin, and Greek translations of Hafiz's odes. Though not exactly faithful to the original Persian text, Jones' translation is graceful and imparts some of the ambience of Hafiz. His rendition of the famous ode beginning "Sweet maid, if thou would'st charm my sight" is included in most anthologies of eighteenth century English poetry. Jones' translation did much to spread the name of Hafiz in the English-speaking world.

After Sir William Jones, there appeared a string of English translations of Hafiz: J. Nott whose *Selected Odes* was released in 1787; T. Ford; T. Law; J. H. Hindly; and Edward Cowell. The best known English translations of Hafiz were done by Gertrude Bell (1897), Walter Leaf (1898), John Payne (1901), and Richard Le Gallienne (1925). In more recent times, the scholarly works of Arthur J. Arberry (1905-69) has greatly bolstered the fame of Hafiz in the West. The translation presented in this volume is the first English rendition of the odes of Hafiz by an Iranian. My father, Dr. Abbas Aryanpur Kashani, has devoted much of the last quarter century studying, translating, and interpreting the poetry of Hafiz. His translation is a faithful rendition and, hopefully, will serve as a new impetus to the study of Hafiz in English.

Hafiz was born in Shiraz, the city of "roses and nightingales", around 1324 A.D. Little reliable information is available about his life. Evidence gleaned from his work and some of the more plausible legends indicate that Hafiz's father, Baha-Oddin, was a native of Isfahan who migrated to Shiraz to escape the Mongol invaders. His mother was probably from Kazerun, a city to the south of Shiraz. While still a boy, Hafiz lost his father. Eventually, poverty drove him to work as an apprentice to a baker. Being a precocious child, however, he was allowed to audit lessons at a school (*maktab*) near the bakery. As years wore on, Hafiz proved himself an outstanding scholar and calligrapher. The pen-name Hafiz (the memorizer) refers to the fact that he had memorized the Qur'an in its entirety. Even though much is not known about his schooling, it is clear that the man who wrote the odes possessed vast knowledge not only in theology, philosophy, literature, and history, but also in the varieties of the human heart.

During his long career as a poet, Hafiz sought the patronage of a number of local rulers. He wrote some of his earliest poems for Abu-Es'Hagh Inju, the ruler of Shiraz and an enlightened man who revered Hafiz. Unfortunately, in 1356, Shiraz was captured by Amir Mubarez, a ruthless and religious fanatic. Amir Mubarez closed taverns and deprecated artists. While poets like Hafiz were in disfavor, religious zealots gained power and oppressed the people in the name of religion. Many of Hafiz's odes criticize the hypocrisy of religious zealots and the tyranny of magistrates and rulers. The famous ode beginning with " *'Ayb-e rendan makon ay zahed-e pakizeh seresht*" exemplifies his attitude toward zealots in lines such as the following:

Pious clergy! Don't mind libertines like me,
For you won't account for other people's sin.

Mind your business, why in others' you'r keen?
What we saw today, its fruit tomorrow see.

v

In another ode, he says:

They closed the tavern door; O'Lord, do not permit.
That they open the door of shame and deceit.

The tyranny of Amir Mubarez alienated the people and led to a rebellion. Amir Mubarez was blinded and deposed and his son, Shah Shoja' (ruled 1358-85) became the ruler of Shiraz. The new ruler restored the favored position of Hafiz at the court. The poet's happy days, however, did not last long. By 1369 for unknown reasons, Hafiz had once again fallen into disfavor.

It was probably during this period that Hafiz looked elsewhere for support. He made a journey to Isfahan and Yazd, perhaps in search of a generous patron. Meanwhile, the far-reaching fame of his poetry brought Hafiz an invitation from Ahmad Jalayer, the ruler of western Iran, to visit his capital, Baghdad. The reasons why the poet did not go are unknown. Later on, he was invited by Mahmud Shah of Deccan to visit India. It is said that Hafiz journeyed overland to the Strait of Hormuz and boarded a ship bound to India. The sea was stormy and Hafiz, it is said, left the ship and traveled back to Shiraz because he preferred terra firma to the vagaries of the sea.

A few years later, Shiraz was invaded by the Scourge of God, Tamerlane (1336-1405). Legend has it that there occured a meeting between this man of the sword and the man of the pen, Hafiz. Tamerlane is said to have upbraided the poet for having written in one of his well-known odes: "If that Shirazi Turk would take my heart into her hand/For the mole on her cheek, I'd given Bukhara and Samarkand." Tamerlane, himself a native of Samarkand, demanded how Hafiz could have the temerity to give such two great cities just for the mole of a Shirazi woman. Hafiz, it is said, answered, "Your Majesty, it is because of such prodigality that I have fallen into such poverty!"

Hafiz died in 1391. He is buried in a garden which in his

honor is called Hafizieh. His mausoleum is one of the major attractions of Shiraz and is often visited by many of his faithful admirers.

The Cannon of Hafiz

It appears that Hafiz was indifferent toward the task of collecting his own poems. After his death, a friend named Golandam compiled the poet's verses and wrote a preface (*dibacheh*). Ironically, the great popularity of Hafiz is a cause of the difficulties associated with his poetry. To impress their buyers with larger editions, unscrupulous copyists included the works of other poets in the *Divan* of Hafiz. Moreover, in later decades some poets circulated their controversial odes under the name of Hafiz in order to escape persecution. Thus, whereas most scholars and experts believe that Hafiz wrote between four-and five-hundred odes (*ghazals*), some editions of the *Divan* contain more than eight-hundred.

Another difficulty with the poems of Hafiz is the insertion of obtrusive lines and the proliferation of verbal variants. Because of carelessness or a desire to inflate the text, a copyist may have added lines composed by other poets. Similarly, ignorance or a desire for novelty may have led a copyist to tamper with the text. As a result, the great demand for the *Divan* caused excessive copying leading to textual corruption.

In the last decades, Hafiz scholars have tried to arrive at a more authentic text by collating the oldest manuscripts of Hafiz. The latest edition of Hafiz's *Divan* released in Tehran in 1967 by Amir Kabir publishing company is probably the best text available in print. It contains four-hundred and fifty eight odes, two legies (*ghasidehs*) thirty-three shorter pieces (*ghat'a*) and forty-two quatrains (*ruba'i*).

The Poetry of Hafiz

In the Persian-speaking world (Iran, Afghanistan, the

southern republics of the Soviet Union, parts of Pakistan, India, Iraq, Turkey, and regions around the southern half of the Persian Gulf) Hafiz is generally regarded as not only as a great poet, but also as a seer, a "tongue of the mysterious" (*lesan ol qayb*) whose poetry is divinely inspired. In addition to those who read his *Divan* for enlightenment and delight, there are many who consult it to find out the future or to receive guidance and solace. Whether it is a journey, an illness, or an important transaction, lovers of Hafiz usually take a *fal* (augury or divination) with the *Divan*: They take up his book, make a wish, close their eyes, open a page at random, and recite the poem on the page. They thus receive a blend of poetic delight, existential guidance, and moral inspiration.

Because it is often mystical, permeated with more than one theme, and laden with associations, the poetry of Hafiz creates an effect far greater than the sum of its parts. It contains layers of Qur'anic and historical allusions. It also contains an idiosyncratic poetic diction such as *sarv* (cypress tree); *mogh* (Magian); *khergheh* (cloak); *kenesht* (church); and *shahid* (beauty). What makes the odes of hafiz unique (and, alas, this aspect of his poetry is hardly translatable) is the beauty of his images, his mellifluous language, and his magical rhythm.

Even though Hafiz's odes defy classification, they can be loosely divided into four types:

1. Lyrics in which the dominant theme is human love and real (as opposed to symbolic) wine.

2. Odes which deal primarily with mystical love and with wine, rose, lover, etc. as symbols.

3. Poems in which Hafiz makes quick shifts from one theme, image, or allusion to another. Like the second type, these deal with mystical love and symbolic wine, but in much more complex fashion. The odes in this group have multiple themes and luxuriant images. These qualities — and their philosophical depth — make such poems appear obscure and multifaceted, at times even "incoherent." For some native readers, these odes serve as inkblots, evoking different intellec-

tual and emotional reactions, depending on the mood of the hour and the personality of the reader.

4. Finally, there are the poems that contain a relatively large dosage of socio-political undertones. These can be ascribed to the various stages of the poet's life, because they reflect particular events or people. Some of these are panegyrics composed in praise of dignitaries and kings. Others are masterly blends of social commentary and criticism hidden underneath a tropebedecked gossamer of references to love, lover, and wine.

Hafiz's critical comments are mainly directed against hypocritical clergy and harsh magistrates. Such comments make probable the stories about his persecution by magistrates and the mullahs and the desecration of his tomb soon after his death. It is not surprising that the poet who wrote lines such as the following had such invertrate enemies:

Hafiz, drink! Sheikh and Sheriff, I tell,
All are hypocrites, if you examine them well!

Or:

It is really better to be a sinner great,
Than worship god in a foreign state.

It is also not surprising that in today's Iran the ruling mullahs have found his poetry objectionable. After a lapse of almost six-hundred years during which Hafiz was revered as a saint once again he has fallen into disfavor with a theocracy that considers his poetry morally and religiously subversive.

HOW TO USE THIS BOOK

If the reader wishes to approximate the experience of the Persian reader who consults Hafiz about life's problems and soothsaying, he/she should proceed as follows: Make a wish, close your eyes, open the book at random, read the poem carefully, and try to understand the message. The interpretations given below each poem are intended to aid the reader in understanding the message of the ode:

Throughout centuries, millions have found answers to their problems in Hafiz's odes. It is hoped that this translation will also impart moral benefits to those who seek their guidance. A reading of the "Terminology of Hafiz" presented here will result in a better understanding of the poetry of Hafiz.

Manoochehr Aryanpur Kashani
Buena Vista College, Iowa
Summer, 1984

THE TERMINOLOGY OF HAFIZ

ABODE OF SORROW. The world.

ALEXANDER'S JAIL. This world.

ALEXANDER'S MIRROR. Alexander the Great was said to have possessed a mirror, like the crystal ball, in which was reflected the whole world. Wherever Hafiz uses this expression he means the wine cup.

ARAK. A city in Iran, formerly known as Sultanabad.

BAGHDAD. A city of ancient Iran, now the capital of Iraq.

BEAUTY. Wherever Hafiz uses the word "beauty", he means God, or sometimes sensory or sensual beauty, or both.

BLUE DOME. Heaven or God.

BUKHARA AND SAMARKAND. Two great cities of ancient Iran,. now in Soviet Union.

BULBUL. The Persian song bird, believed to be a nightingale. Sometimes Hafiz uses this word to mean himself; at other times *bulbul* signifies a true and steadfast lover.

CANDLE AND BUTTERFLY. In Iranian literature, the butterfly is shown to be in great love with the candle, so much so that it burns itself for the love of the candle. It also signifies the true lovers.

CLEAN BREAD. In Islam bread is considered clean, whereas wine and other alcoholic beverages are considered unclean.

CLERGY. The Muslim clergy or *sheikh* whom Hafiz considered sham, without truth. Wherever Hafiz uses the word *sheikh* or clergy he means hypocritical.

CURTAIN HOLDER. The spiritual leaders who stand at the gate of the temple or place of worship and guide people to God. He means in general all religious leaders, who hold the curtain, hiding God and truth from the public.

CYPRESS AND CYPRESS FIGURE. A beautiful and tall girl.

DARIUS. Darius the Great, one of the greatest kings of Iran; also Darius, the last king of the Achaemenian dynasty overthrown by Alexander the Great in 332 B.C.

DARLING. God, and sometimes the carnal beauties.

DERVISH. Persian mystic; also a poor mendicant or beggar.

EARTHLY MOON. A carnal beauty; in particular, Hafiz's beloved.

ETERNAL TEACHER. God.

FARS. A province of Iran from ancient times, from where came the Persians, who ruled over Iran. The Greeks began to use the name "Parse" or "Perse" (Persia) for the whole of ancient Iran, whereas it was the name of only one province. Even up to a few years ago, the Europeans called Iran "Perse" or "Persia" because of this historical error of the Greeks. Hafiz and many other famous poets were born and raised in Shiraz, the capital of Pars or Fars.

FRIEND. Almost everytime Hafiz uses the word "friend" he means God, though sometimes he means a human friend and often times he means both God and a human friend.

GARDENER. God, in the sense used in Ode on page 245.

GRAVE ARCHITECT. God, who has the power over life and death.

HAJI. The title for Muslims who have been on pilgrimage to Mecca (the House of God), in Saudi Arabia at a certain season of the year and performed certain rites. A Muslim must have a certain amount of wealth to be entitled to go on this pilgrimage.

HALLAJ. Name of a person who taught people that everything is divine. He, therefore, declared himself as God, and was put on the gallows for this sacrilege.

HER. The word "her" or "him" and all the other forms of this pronoun can signify both female and male because the Persian third person singular is "oo" (as in *too*) meaning either "he" or "she" or even "it".

HIM. See *her.* Whenever this word is written in capital letters, it means God.

HYPOCRITE. Hafiz uses the word "hypocrite" to mean the Muslim clergy or *sheikh,* who were outwardly very religious, but inwardly full of vices.

JAM. Jam or Jamshid was one of the ancient and legendary kings of Iran.

JAM'S CUP. Jam's cup, or Jamshid's cup, was a cup that belonged to Jam. It is said that Jam's cup reflected the whole. world in it, and like the cystal ball, it could discover many hidden secrets. Hafiz used this phrase to mean the wine cup.

JIN. Fairy, or imaginary being.

JOSEPH-LIKE BEAUTY. Means the beauty of Joseph the son of Jacob, who was favored by Pharaoh. Joseph is said to have been strongly loved by Zulaikha, the queen of Egypt, because of his striking beauty.

JUDGE. God.

LEILY AND MAJNOON. In Iranian and Arabic literature Majnoon was a great lover and Leily was his sweetheart for whose love he wandered in desert and among hills. ,

MAGI-SAGE. The Magi-Sage, wherever used by Hafiz, or "the Sage" means Zoroastrian priests, who were known to be holders of great secrets of truth. Also, because producing and selling wine is forbidden in Islam, usually the non-Muslim such as Zoroastrians, Jews, or Christians made and sold wine. Of course, whenever Hafiz visited the Magi-Sage, he took advantage of the visit and drank wine too, as he could not have it in any Muslim shop.

MAJNOON. See *Leily*.

MASTER. The Creator.

MECCA. The holy shrine of the Muslims, i.e., House of God. The Rich Muslims are expected to make a pilgrimage to this city once in their lifetime at a certain season to perform certain rites. See also *Hajj*.

MOON-FACED. The moon symbolizes great beauty in Iranian art and literature. "Moon-faced" means a beautiful girl.

MOON TO FISH. This expression, as used in ode on page 260, means from the Heavens down to the Earth or from the sky down to the deep seas where the fish live.

NIGHTINGALE. In Iranian literature the nightingale is

deeply in love with the rose. Sometimes Hafiz uses the word to mean "great and devoted lovers," including himself.

PAINTER. God.

PARS. See *Fars.*

PLUNDERING TURKS. During Hafiz's time, the Turks and Monguls had attacked Iran and were plundering most of the cities, showing no mercy to the people. So, like plundering Turks, the eyes of Hafiz's sweetheart, plundered all his heart and patience.

ROSE. See *nightingale.*

RUINED HOME. This world of corruption and death.

SAGE. *Magi-Sage.* It also means a wise person.

SAKI. A waitress who serves wine. In Hafiz's times, as to-day, usually the most charming maids were used as waitresses.

SAMARKAND AND BUKHARA. See *Bukhara.*

SHEIKH. The Muslim clergy, who, to Hafiz, was the symbol of sham and hypocrisy.

SHIRAZ. Capital of Fars or Pars, and one of the ancient cities of Iran. It is the birthplace of Hafiz and Sa'di, two of the greatest Iranian poets. It is also noted for its wine and the captivating eyes of its beautiful women.

SOLOMON'S REALM. As used in Ode on page 230, it means paradise, or the realm of truth.

SUFI. The Muslim mystics who wore coarse, woolen cloaks and spent their time in prayer and incantations, punctuated with intervals of ecstacy.

TABRIZ. Capital of the province of Azarbaijan and an ancient city of Iran.

TAVERN. The abode of the Magi-Sage, where wine was prepared and served. Islam forbids wine drinking and so no Muslim is permitted to prepare and sell it. It also means any worhsipping place such as a church, mosque, pagoda, etc.

TRUE WINE. Hafiz uses the words "wine", "everlasting wine", or "true wine" to mean the Truth, as he explains in Ode on page 136. To Hafiz, wine was the symbol of truth;

for just as wine changes the mood and temper of people, so does truth change souls. Occasionally, of course, the word "wine" is used literally.

UNCLEAN DRINK. Wine and other alcoholic drinks were considered "unclean" by the Muslims.

WINE. See *true wine*.

YAR. Persian word, meaning "friend" or "sweetheart." To Hafiz it generally meant God.

ZULAIKHA. The queen of Egypt who fell in love with Joseph, the son of Jacob.

MAKE A WISH

CLOSE YOUR EYES

OPEN THE BOOK TO ANY PAGE

THEN

READ THE POEM WITH INTERPRETATION

AND

YOU WILL GET YOUR ANSWER

FROM

THE INSPIRED MYSTIC POEMS

OF

HAFIZ

Odes of Hafiz

Poetical Horoscope

Serve the cup around, O'Saki, for love, I say,
Seemed easy first, yet difficult in the end.

Lovers' hearts are bleeding, and sure will rend,
When zephyr spreads scent of her curls away.

In security how can travellers stay,
When trumpets the message of departure send?

The experienced sage, advised us to say, :
"Wash your prayer-rug in red wine, my friend".

Those secure on the shore with peace of mind,
Don't know our storm the waves and the dark night.

Alas, that at last my secrets I find,
Untold at street corners, even before my sight.

Hafiz, enjoy her company and to her bind,
Suffer the dark world for the sake of future light.

INTERPRETATION

*Be happy, though things may seem easy first, yet they will be
more difficult in the end. Your friends cannot appreciate the difficult
situation you are facing. Yet, if you seek success, you must endure
all hardships, for there is hope of great relief for you.*

الا یا ایها الساقی ادر کأساً و ناولها
که عشق آسان نمود اول ولی افتاد مشکلها

به بوی نافه کآخر صبا زان طره بگشاید
ز تاب جعد مشکینش چه خون افتاد در دلها

مرا در منزل جانان چه امن عیش چون هر دم
جرس فریاد می‌دارد که بربندید محملها

به می سجاده رنگین کن گرت پیر مغان گوید
که سالک بی‌خبر نبود ز راه و رسم منزلها

شب تاریک و بیم موج و گردابی چنین هایل
کجا دانند حال ما سبکباران ساحلها

همه کارم ز خود کامی به بدنامی کشید آخر
نهان کی ماند آن رازی کز او سازند محفلها

حضوری گر همی خواهی از او غایب مشو حافظ
متی ما تلق من تهوی دع الدنیا و اهملها

If that Turk of Shiraz would satisfy my heart,
Samarkand and Bukhara I'ld give for her mole.

Saki, serve the lasting wine in whole;
In paradise you won't get.companies so smart!

The exalted musicians well played their part,
Like plundering Turks, our patience they stole.

My meagre love's rejected by my sweetheart,
Before her beauty, my love is a cajole.

Her Joseph-like beauty, could well enchant,
Charming Zulaikha, with a love so strong.

I pray for thee, even if your curse is extant,
Anything is sweet, if expressed by your tongue.

Enjoy wine and music, in every instant,
Hearken the advice of Hafiz, O'fortunate young!

INTERPRETATION

*You are willing to give anything in order to get your desire .
You are very impatient to get what you want. In spite of all injustice
done to you, you still have a kind heart and wish well for your enemies.
Try to forget worries and spend your time in happiness.*

اگر آن ترک شیرازی بدست آرد دل ما را   بخال هندویش بخشم سمرقند و بخارا را

بده ساقی می باقی که در جنت نخواهی یافت   کنار آب رکن آباد و گلگشت مصلا را

فغان کاین لولیان شوخ شیرین کار شهرآشوب   چنان بردند صبر از دل که ترکان خوان یغما را

ز عشق ناتمام ما جمال یار مستغنی است   به آب و رنگ و خال و خط چه حاجت روی زیبا را

من از آن حسن روزافزون که یوسف داشت دانستم   که عشق از پرده عصمت برون آرد زلیخا را

اگر دشنام فرمائی و گر نفرین دعا گویم   جواب تلخ می زیبد لب لعل شکرخا را

نصیحت گوش کن جانا که از جان دوست تردارند   جوانان سعادتمند پند پیر دانا را

حدیث از مطرب و می گو و راز دهر کمتر جو   که کس نگشود و نگشاید به حکمت این معما را

غزل گفتی و در سفتی بیا و خوش بخوان حافظ

که بر نظم تو افشاند فلک عقد ثریا را

Zephyr! Tell that charming gazelle of mine,
"Because of you I wander through desert and hill.

"Have regard for my excitement and thrill;
"Favor me   with your lips—sweet and divine!

"You're so proud, my rose, of that charm of thin‹
"That of your nightingale, you never enquire will.

"Cunning birds aren't caught by trap and skill,
"But by tender love and a temper benign.

"All those claiming beauty and charm,
"Lack loyalty, friendship and devotion.

"When you enjoy drinks with friends kind and warm,
"Remember my love and my tender emotion!"

No loyalty in fine face and tender arm.
Hafiz! Your sweet odes brought angels to motion.

INTERPRETATION

You have been wandering a good deal, seeking your aim. But you must remember that a mild attitude and patience will only enable you to get what you want. Do not expect loyalty and devotion from all who promise you so.

غزلیات حافظ

صبا بلطف بگو آن غزال رعنا را / که سر بکوه و بیابان تو داده‌ای ما را

شکرفروش که عمرش دراز باد چرا / تفقدی نکند طوطی شکرخا را

غرور حسنت اجازت مگر نداد ای گل / که پرسشی نکنی عندلیب شیدا را

بخلق و لطف توان کرد صید اهل نظر / ببند و دام نگیرند مرغ دانا را

ندانم از چه سبب رنگ آشنایی نیست / سهی قدان سیه چشم ماه سیما را

چو با حبیب نشینی و باده پیمایی / بیاد دار محبان بادپیما را

جز این قدر نتوان گفت در جمال تو عیب / که وضع مهر و وفا نیست روی زیبا را

در آسمان نه عجب گر بگفته حافظ

سرود زهره برقص آورد مسیحا را

7

My heart is out of control! Help me out , Sages!
Alas! My secret love 'll be told through ages.

Shipwrecks we are, move on O' breeze!
Perhaps again I can see the friend at ease.

The few-days earthly love, is all dream and romance.
Be kind to friends, now that you've a chance.

"Bring the morning cup", sang last night the Bulbul ,
While surrounded by heaps of flowers and Mul.

In gratitude of your blessings, O' bounteous man !
Help the poor Dervish, as much as you can.

Happiness of the two worlds, but two phrases show: -
"Justice to the friend; compromise to your foe."

Never admitted to mansion of fame and success.
We cannot change destiny, let's all confess.

In time of misfortune, enjoy wine and pleasure,
For thus a beggar gains the hidden treasure.

The wine-cup is like Alexander's mirror, look!
Therein you know Darius's kingdom he took .

Forgive me, O' clean-skirted Sheikh of mine;
It's God's will, if my cloak 's smeared with wine.

INTERPRETATION

*You may be in a difficult position at present; but there is the hope
that a breeze of success will save you from a stormy life. You will
have many blessings, but never forget the poor people. Even in your
greatest success, play fair with your enemies and friends. When you
feel unhappy, cheer up, and never mind, for inside you there is the
hidden treasure of self-contentment.*

دل می‌رود ز دستم صاحب‌دلان خدا را   دردا که راز پنهان خواهد شد آشکارا

کشتی شکسته‌گانیم ای باد شرطه برخیز   باشد که بازبینیم دیدار آشنا را

ده روزه مهر گردون افسانه است و افسون   نیکی به جای یاران فرصت شمار یارا

در حلقه گل و مل خوش خواند دوش بلبل   هات الصبوح حبوا یا ایها السکارا

ای صاحب کرامت شکرانه سلامت   روزی تفقدی کن درویش بی‌نوا را

آسایش دو گیتی تفسیر این دو حرف است   با دوستان مروت با دشمنان مدارا

در کوی نیک‌نامی ما را گذر ندادند   گر تو نمی‌پسندی تغییر کن قضا را

آن تلخ‌وش که صوفی ام الخبائثش خواند   اشهی لنا و احلی من قبلة العذارا

هنگام تنگدستی در عیش کوش و مستی   کاین کیمیای هستی قارون کند گدا را

سرکش مشو که چون شمع از غیرتت بسوزد   دلبر که در کف او موم است سنگ خارا

آیینه سکندر جام می است بنگر   تا بر تو عرضه دارد احوال ملک دارا

خوبان پارسی‌گو بخشندگان عمرند   ساقی بده بشارت رندان پارسا را

حافظ به خود نپوشید این خرقه می آلود

ای شیخ پاک‌دامن معذور دار ما را

Rise! O' Saki! and bring us pure wine,
And help us forget the sorrows of days.

Help us cast away sham's cloak and its ways,
I don't care for fame, though to the wise it's fine.

The smother of my burning heart, though benign,
Burned all withered hearts, with its radiant rays.

My love-frenzied heart cries out and says:
"To whom can I confide my secrets divine?"

I enjoy the blessed company of my sweetheart,
Though she has taken away all my peace of mind.

The cypress, the turf, and all the fine art,
Have no appeal to me, when she's so kind.

O' Hafiz, suffer hardships and be smart;
Some day, at last, your aim you will find.

INTERPRETATION

With high spirits, try to forget your sorrows. Avoid sham and be truthful, for truth has greater effect. You do not seem to appreciate your many blessings, because of certain things you lack, but you must enjoy them all and go on with patience, for at last you will get what you want.

ساقیا برخیز و در ده جام را / خاک بر سر کن غم ایام را

ساغرم ی بر کفم نه تا ز بر / برکشم این دلق ازرق فام را

گر چه بد نامیست نزد عاقلان / ما نمیخواهیم ننگ و نام را

باده در ده چند ازین باد غرور / خاک بر سر نفس نافرجام را

دود آه سینهٔ نالان من / سوخت این افسرده گان خام را

محرم راز دل شیدای خود / کس نمی بینم ز خاص و عام را

با دلارامی مرا خاطر خوشست / کز دلم یکباره برد آرام را

نگرد دیگر به رو اندر چمن / هر که دید آن سرو سیم اندام را

صبر کن حافظ بسختی روز و شب / عاقبت روزی بیابی کام را

Good news: to the sweet-singing nightingale!
For the garden is full of life once again.

Zephyr! When you pass by the turf and plain,
Convey my message to buds and flowers frail: -

"Since so charming is that wine-serving female,
"At the tavern threshold I' ll always remain.

"Darling! Thy love made me errant with pain;
"In thy bosom—as in Noah's Ark— I safely sail."

Those condemning the drinkers, I am afraid,
Their piety and faith at tavern will stake.

Since in grave all our bodies will be laid,
Why then greedy plans we attempt to make?

Hafiz! Drink and be the robbers' aid,
But evil advantage of religion never take.

INTERPRETATION

Good news for you! Once more there is success for you. After a series of hard efforts, you are now successful and feel secure in every respect. Many people who condemned your activities, are now following in your footsteps. Nevertheless, do not make yourself too much involved in greedy plans, realising that life is short and that the best should be made of your present time.

رونق عهد شباب است دگر بستان را ** میرسد مژده که ایام غم نخواهد ماند چنان را

ای صبا گر بجوانان چمن باز رسی ** خدمت ما برسان سرو و گل و ریحان را

گر چنین جلوه کند مغبچه باده فروش ** خاکروب در میخانه کنم مژگان را

ای که بر مه کشی از عنبر سارا چوگان ** مضطرب حال مگردان من سرگردان را

ترسم این قوم که بر درد کشان می‌خندند ** در سر کار خرابات کنند ایمان را

یار مردان خدا باش که در کشتی نوح ** هست خاکی که بآبی نخرد طوفان را

برو از خانه گردون بدر و نان مطلب ** کان سیه کاسه در آخر بکشد مهمان را

هر که را خوابگه آخر مشتی خاک است ** گو چه حاجت که بافلاک کشی ایوان را

ماه کنعانی من مسند مصر آن تو شد ** وقت آن است که بدرود کنی زندان را

حافظا می خور و رندی کن و خوش باش ولی ** دام تزویر مکن چون دگران قرآن را

Brethren of faith: What shall we hereafter do ?
Our leader left the mosque for tavern yesterday!

How can followers turn to Mecca to pray?
When our leader has the tavern in view?

The joy of her love if sanity ever knew,
Like us insanes in fetters of her curls 'd stay.

Destiny forced us spend our lives this way:
We believe in fate and hold it to be true.

Your beautiful face displayed a new grace.
That's why I see nothing, but grace and good.

Does my fiery sigh and its burning trace,
Affect your stone-heart? I wonder if it would!

Hafiz, your sighs' darts pierced sky and space!
How my friend such piercing darts withstood?

INTERPRETATION

If your leader changes sides, never mind. You stick to your side and be steadfast. You have seen enough blessings on your side to remain faithful to it all your life.You may feel disappointed that your efforts have been ignored by your superiors, but this is not so.

غزلیات حافظ

وزش از مسجد سوی میخانه آمد پیرما
چیست یاران طریقت بعد ازین تدبیرها

ما مریدان روی سوی قبله چون آریم چون
روی سوی خانه خمار دارد پیرما

در خرابات طریقت ما بهم منزل شویم
کاین چنین رفتست در عهد ازل تقدیرها

عقل اگر داند که دل دربند زلفش چون خوشست
عاقلان دیوانه گردند از پی زنجیرها

روی خوبت آیتی از لطف بر ما کشف کرد
زان زمان جز لطف و خوبی نیست در تفسیرها

با دل سنگینت آیا هیچ درگیرد شبی
آه آتشناک و سوز سینهٔ شبگیرها

تیر آه ما زگردون بگذرد حافظ خموش
رحم کن بر جان خود پرهیز کن از تیرها

Saki! Brighten our cups with the wine so bright!
Call musicians: The world turns to our favor right.

O' ignorant of our permanent pleasure in wine!
I take wihe, for friend's reflection therein shine.

In the world chronicles, eternal is my name.
One never dies, whose heart is with love aflame.

Zephyr, if you ever pass by my friend,
This message to her I desire to send: -

"Why deliberately try to forget my name?
"A time will come when you won't recall same."

It's good to be mellow with the eyes of the friend,
That's why I chose drinking as my end.

The Sheik's "clean bread" and my "unclean drink"
Will earn the same, on resurrection, I think.

Hafiz, wipe off your tears, since you'll get,
The bird of happiness, entrapped in your net.

INTERPRETATION

Be happy, for you are successful, and things move in your favor.
Cheer up, for happiness and success will come to you soon.

ساقی به نور باده برافروز جام ما / مطرب بگو که کار جهان شد به کام ما

ما در پیاله عکس رخ یار دیده‌ایم / ای بی‌خبر ز لذت شرب مدام ما

هرگز نمیرد آنکه دلش زنده شد به عشق / ثبت است بر جریده عالم دوام ما

چندان بود کرشمه و ناز سهی قدان / کاید به جلوه سرو صنوبر خرام ما

ای باد اگر به گلشن احباب بگذری / زنهار عرضه ده بر جانان پیام ما

گو نام ما ز یاد به عمدا چه می‌بری / خود آید آنکه یاد نیاری ز نام ما

مستی به چشم شاهد دلبند ما خوش است / زان رو سپرده‌اند به مستی زمام ما

ترسم که صرفه‌ای نبرد روز بازخواست / نان حلال شیخ ز آب حرام ما

حافظ ز دیده دانه اشکی همی‌فشان / باشد که مرغ وصل کند قصد دام ما

دریای اخضر فلک و کشتی هلال / هستند غرق نعمت حاجی قوام ما

The curve of thy brow, O' beloved sweetheart!
Hits my poor heart, like a piercing dart.

There was no creation, when there was love.
Love is an old masterpiece of Heaven above.

If narcissus made amour only by chance,
Your enchanting eyes caused wars by a glance.

When I passed through the turf last night,
The buds reminded me of your mouth so tight.

The violets moved by zephyr, fresh and gay,
Refreshed my memory of your curls' display.

I'm now washing my cloak in clear wine;
I can't get away from this destiny of mine.

Hafiz, by enduring love you gain success.
This is eternal destiny, let's all confess.

The globe now turns to my heart's desire,
Since her eternal beauty I really admire.

INTERPRETATION

Many troubles have come to you from friends, but you must suffer them all with great patience, since only by enduring them you will gain success. Be sure, success will come to you in the end and you will be happy.

نمی‌که ابروی شوخ تو در کمان انداخت / بقصد جان من زار ناتوان انداخت

نبود نقش دو عالم که رنگ الفت بود / زمانه طرح محبت نه این زمان انداخت

بیک کرشمه که نرگس بخود فروشی کرد / فریب چشم تو صد فتنه در جهان انداخت

شراب خورده و خوی کرده میروی بچمن / که آب روی تو آتش در ارغوان انداخت

بگردنا گه چمن دوش مست بگذشتم / چو از دهان توام غنچه در گمان انداخت

بنفشه طره مفتول خود گره میزد / صبا حکایت زلف تو در میان انداخت

ز شرم آنکه بروی تو نسبتش کردم / سمن بدست صبا خاک در دهان انداخت

من از ورع می و مطرب بدی نمی‌دیدم / هوای نفس بچکانم در این و آن انداخت

کنون بآب می لعل خرقه میشویم / نصیبه ازل از خود نمی توان انداخت

مگر گشایش حافظ در این خرابی بود / که بخشش ازل رطل در مغان انداخت

جهان بکام من اکنون شود که دور زمان / مرا به بندگی خواجه جهان انداخت

19

The love of my friend set my heart to fire –
A fire that burns my existence entire.

My body smelt from separation of the friend.
My soul consumes! What's my sacred love's end?

The burning candle having pitied me last night,
Burned entirely, sympathising my agony and fright.

My piety was at stake by the tavern wine ––
A wine that destroyed all faculties of mine.

I broke repentance, when I broke wine-glass.
My heart's aching without wine, alas !

Come close, my friend, and tell me no tale.
My eyes seek your sight, with pain and ail.

Hafiz, keep still, and drink the wine deep;
The candle burned all night and you didn't sleep.

INTERPRETATION

*You seem to be bothered and troubled with certain worries. You
have tried many times to keep away from something you really like
to do, but you can not keep yourself from not doing it. You have
broken your repentance many times. No matter what may happen,
you are still attached to what you like, even though this may cost
you very dear. But be happy, for in the nights of your worries, the
candle of relief will burn.*

سینه از آتش دل در غم جانانه بسوخت   آتشی بود در این خانه که کاشانه بسوخت

تنم از واسطه دوری دلبر گداخته است   جانم از آتش مهر رخ جانانه بسوخت

سوز دل بین که ز بس آتش اشکم دل شمع   دوش بر من ز سر مهر چو پروانه بسوخت

آشنائی نه غریب است که دلسوز من است   چون من از خویش نرفتم دل بیگانه بسوخت

فکر توبه مرا آب خرابات ببرد   خانه عقل مرا آتش میخانه بسوخت

چون پیاله دلم از توبه که کردم بشکست   ماجرا کم کن و باز آگر مرا مردم چشم

لاله جگرم بی غم خانه بسوخت   فکر این غصه بدرآور و دیگر از بسوخت

ترک افسانه بگو حافظ و می نوش دمی   که نخفتیم شب و شمع بافسانه بسوخت

Take me to my friend, O' the Dawn Breeze!
Where that killer of lovers, now stays at ease?

In a gloomy night we're on the way to rescue.
O' divine light ! Lead me to the rendez-vous.

All coming to this world, have a sad end;
Why then in the tavern, soberness pretend?

If you wonder where is entrapped my heart -
Watch her curly hair and her looks so smart.

The musicians, the Saki and wine are ready for me.
These are no good without her. Where's she?

Hafiz! Of the autumn wind be not forlorn.
Be reasonable. There's no rose without a thorn.

INTERPRETATION

*You are very ambitious to get what you desire, at all costs.
Though things look dark and gloomy to you now, don't be disappointed
for a divine light of salvation will save you. All the means of happiness
are ready for you, but you do not seem to enjoy them without getting
what you want. But remember, just as the autumn ends with the
spring, so your disappointments will end to a happy and prosperous
future.*

ای نسیم سحر آرامگه یار کجاست   منزل آن ماه عاشق کش عیار کجاست

شب تار است و ره وادی ایمن در پیش   آتش طور کجا موعد دیدار کجاست

هر که آمد به جهان نقش خرابی دارد   در خرابات بگویید که هشیار کجاست

آنکس است اهل بشارت که اشارت داند   نکته ها هست بسی محرم اسرار کجاست

هر سر موی مرا با تو هزاران کار است   ما کجاییم و ملامتگر بیکار کجاست

باز پرسید ز گیسوی شکن در شکنش   کاین دل غمزده سرگشته گرفتار کجاست

عقل دیوانه شد آن سلسله مشکین کو   دل ز ما گوشه گرفت ابروی یار کجاست

حافظ از باد خزان در چمن دهر مرنج

فکر معقول بفرما گل بی خار کجاست

23

When judging lovers don't say "They are astray".
You're not qualified to judge them, my son.

Who is within me, when I'm alone,
That though I'm still, it cries away?

I never care for the world's pleasures, anyway.
Except when her beauty shines as the Sun.

Soaked in heart-blood are the monk and the nun.
They should purify themselves with wine, I pray.

I'm so respected at the Magi's fire-altar,
Because the everlasting fire burns inside me.

What a tune the musician played with her guitar!
My heart recalls; though things pass as you see.

Last night your love message reached me from afar;
For which reason my heart is full of glee.

INTERPRETATION

*You must be very fair in your judgement about things and people.
Everybody has his own problems and worries.You are well received
in certain places because of your straight-forward manners. Keep this
up.Soon you will hear some good news which will make you very
happy.*

چو بشنوی سخن اهل دل مگو که خطاست   سخن شناس نه‌ای جان من خطا اینجاست

سرم به دنیی و عقبی فرو نمی‌آید   تبارک الله از این فتنه‌ها که در سر ماست

در اندرون من خسته دل ندانم کیست   که من خموشم و او در فغان و در غوغاست

دلم ز پرده برون شد کجایی ای مطرب   بنال هان که از این پرده کار ما به نواست

مرا به کار جهان هرگز التفات نبود   رخ تو در نظر من چنین خوشش آراست

نخفته‌ام ز خیالی که می‌پزد دل من   خمار صد شبه دارم شرابخانه کجاست

چنین که صومعه آلوده شد ز خون دلم   گرم به باده بشویید حق به دست شماست

از آن به دیر مغانم عزیز می‌دارند   که آتشی که نمیرد همیشه در دل ماست

چه ساز بود که در پرده می‌زد آن مطرب   که رفت عمر و هنوزم دماغ پر ز هواست

ندای عشق تو دیشب در اندرون دادند

فضای سینه حافظ هنوز پر ز صداست

Sweetheart! I think of thee all the time!
Your perfumed curls refresh my lonely soul.

Witness my love, your beauty and your mole.
Claiming indifference to your love is a crime.

The apple-of-your-chin, expresses a fact sublime: -
"Thousands of lovers fall deep in this hole."

Bad-luck and short arms, deprived me of my goal,
So I couldn't reach her long tresses in time.

Tell the gate-keeper of your intimate heart,
To admit this lover who is sincere and true.

Hafiz knocks rarely and will not depart,
Answer him once a year; that will do.

My heart cherishes your love and cunning art -
Though I may often lose sight of you.

INTERPRETATION

The thought of your ambitions gives you great strength to carry on. You have missed your goal once in the past, but are seeking a chance another time. Keep on seeking, and you will get it. You may often think you are working in vain, but keep on trying and you will get what you want.

خیال روی تو در هر طریق همره ماست
نسیم موی تو پیوند جان آگه ماست

برغم مدعیانی که منع عشق کنند
جمال چهرهٔ تو حجت موجه ماست

ببین که سیب زنخدان تو چه میگوید
هزار یوسف مصری فتاده در چه ماست

اگر به زلف دراز تو دست ما نرسد
گناه بخت پریشان و دست کوته ماست

بحاجب در خلوت سرای خاص بگو
فلان ز گوشه نشینان خاک درگه ماست

بصورت از نظر ما اگر چه محجوب است
همیشه در نظر خاطر مرفه ماست

اگر به سالی حافظ دری زند بگشای
که سالهاست که مشتاق روی چون مه ماست

27

With dishevelled hair, smiling lips and drunken state,
With deft skirt, singing lips and cup in hand;

With quarrelsome eyes her sweet lips gave a command,
As she sat beside me at midnight late.

In a melancholy tune she addressed me straight: -
"You and sleep? My lover? I reprimand.

"Such midnight sip, sacrifice will demand,
"Or you'll be profane to love, any rate."

O' pious clergy! Drinkers are not to blame;
For at eternity this was to be their lot.

What God poured in our cup we took same;
Never mind, if from Heaven or Hell we got.

Her tresses and the wine-cup, what a shame!
Broke Hafiz's repentance on the spot.

INTERPRETATION

If you want to succeed, you must be prepared for self-sacrifice. Take things easy, and enjoy whatever comes to you. You may change your mind, against your will.

زلف آشفته و خوی کرده و خندان لب و مست / پیرهن چاک و غزلخوان و صراحی در دست

نرگسش عربده جوی و لبش افسوس کنان / نیم شب دوش ببالین من آمد بنشست

سر فرا گوش من آورد بآواز حزین / گفت ای عاشق دیرینه من خوابت هست

عاشقی را که چنین باده شبگیر دهند / کافر عشق بود گر نشود باده پرست

برو ای زاهد و بر دردکشان خرده مگیر / که ندادند جز این تحفه بما روز الست

آنچه او ریخت بپیمانه ما نوشیدیم / اگر از خمر بهشتست و گر باده مست

خنده جام می و زلف گره گیر نگار
ای بسا توبه که چون توبه حافظ بشکست

29

I swear to Hafiz's loyalty, honest and true,
That my morning prayers are all for you .

My tears shedding like Noah's storm.
Can't wash your love away from my form .

Buy my broken heart. Yes, make a deal-
The purest heart it will sure reveal.

My heart ! don't expect her profound grace .
Where there's love, selfishness has no place .

Be true, for truth makes your words shine .
Lie blackens the beautiful face of thine.

I'm a wanderer through the desert and hill,
But my troubled heart, you don't pity still.

Hafiz! There's no loyalty in beauty,
Withered trees give gardener no duty.

INTERPRETATION

*You have a pure heart and great ambition. But if you seek success,
you must work hard with unselfishness, and must be truthful to the end.
But meantime you should not expect the impossible to happen. If
you only do your best, that will do.*

بجان خواجه و حق قدیم و عهد درست   که مونس دم صبحم دعای دولت تست
سرشک من که ز طوفان نوح دست برد   ز لوح سینه نیارست نقش مهر تو شست
بکن معامله وین دل شکسته بخر   که باشکستگی ارزد بصد هزار درست
زبان مور بآصف دراز گشت و رواست   که خواجه خاتم جم یافت و بازجست
دلا طمع مبر از لطف بی نهایت دوست   چو لاف عشق زدی سر باز چالاک و چست
بصدق کوش که خورشید زاید از نفست   که از دروغ سیه روی گشت صبح نخست
شدم ز دوست توبید ای کوه و دشت هنوز   نمی کنی تو ترحم نطاق سلسله ست

مرنج حافظ و از دلبران حفاظ مجوی
گناه باغ چه باشد چو این گیاه نرست

I don't care for wine when I think of thee;
Let wine barrels go and the tavern mess.

Even if it's paradise wine, spill it in distress,
For the wine is a bore when absent is she.

Alas! My friend is gone with her memory.
On my tearful eyes no design can impress.

Beware my eyes! I'm not secure I guess,
While floods of tears flow and inundate me.

My friend passes unveiled freely before you,
Only to strangers like me she covers her face.

The fields are green, so let us not woe,
Take wine, for mirages are Time and Space.

Hafiz is a libertine but a lover true.
Is love confined to youth and grace?

INTERPRETATION

*When you strive for your aim, you don't care for anything else.
What you try to get, other persons already possess, but don't worry
for, the "fields are green", which means everything is ripe and ready
for your action. Never think for a moment that what you want to get
is confined to certain people; you can also have it if you try.*

32

ما را از خیال تو چه پروای شرابست
خم گو سر خود گیر که خمخانه خرابست

گر خمر بهشت است بریز ید که بی دوست
هر شربتی که دهی عین عذابست

افسوس که شد دلبر و در دیده گریان
تحریر خیال خط او نقش بر آبست

بیدار شوای دیده که ایمن نتوان بود
زین سیل دمادم که در این منزل خوابست

معشوق عیان می گذرد بر تو ولیکن
اغیار همی بیند از آن بسته نقابست

گل بر رخ رنگین تو تا لطف عرق دید
در آتش شوق از غم دل غرق گلابست

سبزست در و دشت بیا تا نگذاریم
دست از سر آبی که جهان جمله سرابست

دریغ و درد ماغم مطلب جای نصیحت
کاین گوشه پر از زمزمه چنگ و ربابست

حافظ چه شد ار عاشق و رند است و نظر باز
بس طور عجب لازم ایام شبابست

The pupil of my eye is your welcome nest;
Step in and dwell therein– it's your place.

O' Nightingale! Enjoy the rose of her face;
Your love-song is heard at the turf with zest.

Your tender lips heal my sickness the best,
Precious rubies are in your treasury of grace.

My body may not have you always to embrace;
My heart is always at your threshold at rest.

My heart would never a cheap love allow.
The treasury of my heart 's sealed with your name.

If the world loves her, the world I'm to follow.
If Heaven is in love, Hafiz is not to blame.

Hafiz, your poetry puts Heaven aglow.
Only such sweet poetry befits your fame.

INTERPRETATION

You are expecting a great thing to happen. But must enjoy the great blessings you have at present. You must try to make the most of your existing blessings. Since everybody has blessings and short-comings, then you should be content with all that you have. You seem to be very steadfast and consistent in your plans.

رواق منظر چشم من آشیانهٔ توست   کرم نما و فرود آ که خانه خانهٔ توست

به لطف خال و خط از عارفان ربودی دل   لطیفه‌های عجب زیر دام و دانهٔ توست

دلت به وصل گل ای بلبل صبا خوش باد   که در چمن همه گلبانگ عاشقانهٔ توست

علاج ضعف دل ما به لب حوالت کن   که این مفرح یاقوت در خزانهٔ توست

من ار چه نیستم از دولت ملازمت   ولی خلاصهٔ جان خاک آستانهٔ توست

من آن نیم که دهم نقد دل به هر شوخی   در خزانه به مهر تو و نشانهٔ توست

تو خود چه لعبتی ای شهسوار شیرین کار   که توسنی چو فلک رام تازیانهٔ توست

چه جای من که بلغزد سپهر شعبده‌باز   از این حیل که در انبانه بهانهٔ توست

سرود مجلست اکنون فلک به رقص آرد

که شعر حافظ شیرین سخن ترانهٔ توست

Come! On the whim's palace don't depend.
Serve wine. for your life will soon end.

I'm the slave of him, who under blue sky,
Is entirely free from all possessions' tie.

When at the tavern last night, was drunk and gay,
I heard the angels good tidings to say:

"O' ambitious falcon, don't fly so high,
"Your nest is the abode of sorrow and sigh".

From Heaven's turret was announced this call: -
"This carnal snare doesn't fit you at all."

Remember my son! Never worry over sorrow,
For passing troubles of today and tomorrow.

"Clear up your frowns" says the inner voice,
"Be happy with your lot: there's no other choice."

Don't seek much loyalty from Time and Tide;
For to many grooms this world-hag was bride.

There's no loyalty in the rose's smile.
O' heartless nightingale! your cry lasts awhile.

Don't be jealous of Hafiz's fluent verse.
It's a gift of the founder of universe.

INTERPRETATION

Avoid whims and work on sure ground. Though you must have high aims and ambitions yet you must be careful not to go too far with your ambitions. After all, there are limited possibilities in this world. But don't forget: Never remain unhappy for what happens today and for what will happen tomorrow. Contentment gives you great happiness. You are not the only one who has not achieved what he desires; numerous others have had similar fates and will have it. Happiness and sorrow both pass away quickly, and so take things easy and stay happ

بیا که قصر امل سخت سست بنیادست
بیار باده که بنیاد عمر بر بادست

غلام همت آنم که زیر چرخ کبود
زهر چه رنگ تعلق پذیرد آزادست

گرت هوای وصالست خاطر ای رخساری
که خاطر از همه غمها بمهر او شادست

چه گویمت که بمیخانه دوش مست و خراب
سروش عالم غیبم چه مژده ها دادست

که ای بلند نظر شاهباز سدره نشین
نشیمن تو نه این کنج محنت آبادست

ترا ز کنگرهٔ عرش می زنند صفیر
ندانمت که در این دامگه چه افتادست

نصیحتی کنمت یاد گیر و در عمل آر
که این حدیث ز پیر طریقتم یادست

غم جهان مخور و پند من مبر از یاد
که این لطیفه عشقم ز ره روی یادست

رضا بداده بده وز جبین گره بگشای
که بر من و تو در اختیار نگشادست

مجو درستی عهد از جهان سست نهاد
که این عجوز عروس هزار دامادست

نشان عهد و وفا نیست در تبسم گل
بنال بلبل بیدل که جای فریادست

حسد چه میبری ای سست نظم بر حافظ
قبول خاطر و لطف سخن خدا دادست

Thank God! The tavern door is open still.
And I can go there when I am in need.

Even wine barrels are drunk there, indeed —
With "the wine of truth" that falsehood will kill.

In my darling you see, vanity and cunning skill,
In me you'll find meakness and humble plead.

I tell her a secret, if she would carefully heed:
Though to no one else, I'd disclose at will: -

I have divorced all happiness and fun ,
Since my eyes witnessed your face and your charm.

Whosoever to your Mecca worship has begun,
Falls on his knees before your seducing charm.

Though like the candle Hafiz will be gone,
His consuming love is still so warm.

INTERPRETATION

*You may feel that those with whom you deal are a little unkind
to you in spite of your kindness. You seem to have concentrated too
much on what you want to get. You are willing to run all risks but
rest assured that your efforts will be fruitful, though a little later than
they should.*

الـمنتـه نقد که در میکده‌ها بارست — زان‌که وکه مرا بر در او روی نیازست

غم‌ها همه در جوشش و خروشند رستی — وآن می که در آبناست حقیقت مجاز

ازوی همه مستی و غرور درست وتکبر — وزما همه بیچارگی و عجز و نیازست

رازی که بر غیر نگفتیم و نگوییم — با دوست بگوییم که او محرم رازست

شرح شکن زلف خم اندر خم جانان — کوته نتوان کرد که این قصه درازست

بار دل مجنون و خم طرّه لیلی — رخساره محمود و کف پای ایازست

بردوختـه‌ام دیده و چو باز از همه عالم — تا دیده به من کبرخ زیبای تو بازست

در کعبه کوی تو هر آنکس که بیاید — از قبلـه ابرو روی تو دین نمازست

ای مجلسیان سوز دل حافظ مسکین — از شمع بپرسید که در سوز و گدازست

Zephyr brings flowers and wine brings fun,
Lyre calls you to drink, beware the Sheriff, my son.

Enjoy wine, a beauty and a book of rhyme,
Behave wisely for seditious is the Time.

Under your old cloak hide the cup with skill,
For soon treacherous Time your blood 'll spill.

To forgive your wine—drink, shed some tears;
For it's fasting time when the hypocrite appears.

No happiness evolves from revolving universe;
Like wine barrel, has dregs on the reverse.

The lofty sky remains – tyrants remain no more,
Their particles in the mud are all in store.

Hafiz your verse took Arak and Fars with ease,
It's now your turn for Baghdad and Tabriz.

INTERPRETATION

Good news are coming to you and you should be very happy with them. Enjoy them all, for happiness passes quickly. In order to be able do what you like, you must sometime do what others like to do. After these happy days, you must expect days full of worry, for such is the attitude of the world. You have gained two successes now and expect two more to come.

اگر چه باده فرح‌بخش و باد گل‌بیزست   به بانگ چنگ مخور می که محتسب تیزست

صراحی‌ای و حریفی گرت به چنگ افتد   بعقل نوش که ایام فتنه انگیزست

در آستین مرقع پیاله پنهان کن   که همچو چشم صراحی زمانه خونریزست

به آب دیده بشوییم خرقه‌ها از می   که موسم ورع و روزگار پرهیزست

مجوی عیش خوش از دور باژگون سپهر   که صاف این سر خم جمله دردی‌آمیزست

سپهر بر شد و پرویزنیست خون افشان   که ریزه‌اش سر کسری و تاج پرویزست

عراق و فارس گرفتی به شعر خوش حافظ

بیا که نوبت بغداد و وقت تبریزست

The rose has the opaque wine-cup in hand;
The nightingale adores it in a lovely tongue.

Stroll on the fields with a book of love-song,
For seminars at this time there's no demand.

The judge (though drunk) issued last night this command:
"Drinking's bad, embezzling bequests is wrong!"

You're destined this wine, but not for long;
Enjoy, therefore, the wine and music band.

Keep away from men and seclusion take,
For it will bring you piety and good name.

If you want to know what the clergy'll make:
Do gold-smith and mat-weaver earn the same?

Keep these secrets, Hafiz, for wisemen's sake,
For as gold they are the old Sage's aim.

INTERPRETATION

Now that you are successful, many people open their mouths to praise you. Don't work too hard, but have some fun too. Since life is short and chances are rare, enjoy, therefore, everything to the best of your ability. Meantime, you must often live alone and think about your life, making necessary plans. Be sure that your efforts will not be futile, and that you will reap the fruits of your endeavors and hard work. But be fair, and expect only results proportionate to your efforts.

کنون که بر کف گل جام باده صاف است
بصد هزار زبان بلبلش در اوصاف است

بخواه دفتر اشعار و راه صحرا گیر
چه وقت مدرسه و بحث کشف کشاف است

فقیه مدرسه دی مست بود و فتوی داد
که می حرام ولی به ز مال اوقاف است

به دُرد و صاف ترا حُکم نیست خوش درکش
که هر چه ساقی ما کرد عین الطاف است

ببُر ز خلق و چو عنقا قیاس کار بگیر
که صیت گوشه نشینان ز قاف تا قاف است

حدیث مدعیان و خیال همکاران
همان حکایت زرد و زبور یا باف است

خموش حافظ و این نکته های چون زر سرخ
نگاه دار که قلاب شهر صرّاف است

A book of verses and a cup of pure wine,
Are truly your most intimate friends.

Watch your road for it has curves and bends;
Enjoy wine for only once is life thine.

If you're learned, óf your learning show a sign,
For wisdom without action the sage evil portends.

In wisdom's eye the world and all its ends,
Are but vague dreams, though appearing very fine.

Without you my heart is sore and frail,
Alas, only death separates me from my friend.

Stick to her tresses and tell no tale,
For good and evil on our stars depend.

Drink eternal wine Hafiz and ne'er fail,
Not even one moment in soberness to spend.

INTERPRETATION

Knowledge and happiness are your best friends. Watch for the curves on the road of your life, but meantime be happy, for only once you are permitted to live in this world. You must try to put your knowledge to action. Hold fast to what you are doing and do your best, depending on luck for what you cannot do. Try always to be happy and never worry.

درین زمانه رفیقی که خالی از خلل است	صراحی می ناب و سفینه غزل است

جریده رو که گذرگاه عافیت تنگ است	پیاله گیر که عمر عزیز بی بدل است

نه من زبی عملی در جهان ملولم و بس	ملالت علما هم ز علم بی عمل است

بچشم عقل درین رهگذار پر آشوب	جهان و کار جهان بی ثبات و بی محل است

بگیر طره مه چهره و قصه مخوان	که سعد و نحس ز تأثیر زهره و زحل است

دلم امید فراوان بوصل روی تو داشت	ولی اجل بره عمر رهزن امل است

بهیچ دور نخواهند یافت هشیارش
چنین که حافظ ما مست باده ازل است

The love of beauties has long been my creed,
A torturing love is the comfort of my life.

Soul-piercing eyes see her beauty in whole-
It isn't the task of mortal eyes indeed.

Remain my friend, for your friendship I need,
For your moon-face my tears—like stars—roll.

Your love played, in my verse, a mighty role;
For this reason people my poetry 'll read.

Grant me the wealth of poverty, O' Lord!
For it brings me true wisdom and glory.

O' friend of sheriff, your vanity I can't afford;
My heart 's the king's mansion, though full o'worry.

Hafiz, of Shirin's love, speak no word,
My friend's sweet lips explain my love story.

INTERPRETATION

You are steadfast in your career even though it has brought you many inconveniences. You must have much deeper insight in order to understand things connected with your life. Although you are to have ambition, yet do not concentrate all your efforts on the accumulation of wealth. On the contrary, try to increase your knowledge and insight. Although you are much troubled, yet a great honor will be bestowed on you soon.

روزگارسیت که سودای بتان دین منست غم این کار نشاط دل غمگین منست

دیدن روی ترا دیده جان بین باید وین کجا مرتبه چشم جهان بین منست

یار من باشش که زیب فلک و زینت دهر از مه روی تو و اشک چو پروین منست

تا مراعشق تو تعلیم سخن گفتن کرد خلق را ورد زبان مدحت و تحسین منست

دولت فقر خدایا بمن ارزانی دار کین کرامت سبب حشمت و تمکین منست

واعظ شحنه شناس این عظمت کو مفروش زانکه منزلگه سلطان دل مسکین منست

یا رب این کعبه مقصود تماشا گه کیست که مغیلان طریقش گل و نسرین منست

حافظ از حشمت پرویز دگر قصه مخوان که لبش جرعه کش خسرو شیرین منست

غزلیات حافظ

منم که گوشهٔ میخانه خانقاه منست
دعای پیر مغان ورد صبحگاه منست

گرم ترانهٔ چنگ صبوح نیست چه باک
نوای من بسحر آه عذرخواه منست

ز پادشاه و گدا فارغم بحمدالله
گدای خاک در دوست پادشاه منست

غرض ز مسجد و میخانه‌ام وصال شماست
جز این خیال ندارم خدا گواه منست

مگر به تیغ اجل خیمه برکنم ورنی
رمیدن از در دولت نه رسم و راه منست

از آن زمان که بر این آستان نهادم روی
فراز مسند خورشید تکیه‌گاه منست

گناه اگر چه نبود اختیار ما حافظ
تو در طریق ادب باش گو گناه منست

In a corner of the tavern forever I retire.
In morning prayers success of the Sage I wish.

Never mind! if music and wine can't replenish.
Only morning sighs for condolence I require.

Neither poverty nor kingdom, o' Lord, I aspire.
Those devoted to her as kings I cherish.

I seek God, whether in mosque or tavern flourish;
God is my witness, nothing else I desire.

Unless the death-sword cuts my tabernacle away
I would never forsake fortune's gate.

Since I faced towards his threshold today;
I feel lofty as the Sun—that's my state!

Hafiz, if sin was not your choice, you say.
For politeness sake, your sins promulgate.

INTERPRETATION

If you don't get what you work hard for, keep working hard and pray, and, you will get it. If you trust the Lord, poverty or wealth will make no real difference for you. Since you are trusting the Lord, you will succeed, and, working hard, you will have a very lofty position, which will be very outstanding. Meantime, do not fail to confess your past mistakes and to correct them by your future deeds.

The sanctuary of God's love is my meagre heart,
My eyes reflect beauties of my sweetheart.

Secrets of two worlds I can never trace,
Only from God I should ask mercy and grace.

Sheikh wants paradise tree; I want the friend.
According to their merits people comprehend.

O' Sheikh, if my skirt's full of filth 'n' dirt,
We are both aware of the friend's clean skirt.

All the flowers that decorate the meadow,
By God's tender love are made to grow.

Now is our turn; bygone is the lover Majnoon,
Every one has few days that expire soon.

All love's kingdom and the treasures of joy,
I received through God's grace, O Boy.

Never mind, if Hafiz's poverty is beyond measure,
God's love has changed his heart to treasure.

INTERPRETATION

It is impossible for you to discover the secrets of God's creation. All you can do is to ask mercy and grace from God. If you have short-comings, never mind, for God will help you. You have your chance now and will enjoy success for some time, but this will pass; so . God's grace will bring you a great deal of riches and joy. With all your poverty and lack of means, God will help you to be rich.

دل سراپردهٔ محبت اوست   دیده آئینه دار طلعت اوست

من که سر درنیاورم بدوکون   گردنم زیر بار منت اوست

تو و طوبی و ما و قامت یار   فکر هر کس بقدر همت اوست

گر من آلوده دامنم چه عجب   همه عالم گواه عصمت اوست

هرگل نو که شد چمن آرای   زاثر رنگ و بوی صحبت اوست

ملکت عاشقی و گنج طرب   هرچه دارم ز ارم زمین همت اوست

من و دل گر فدا شدیم چه باک   غرض اندر میان سلامت اوست

فقر ظاهر مبین که حافظ را

سینه گنجینهٔ محبت اوست

O' Zephyr: If you pass by the realm of my "Y ar"
Bring me the scent of her perfumed tress.

I give my life for her, I declare and confess,
In exchange for a message Zephyr brings from afar.

If I missed her company through unlucky star,
Convey her dust to me and my eyes bless.

What a vague hope: A Dervish and in distress,
I can only dream of her! I'm bizarre.

My oak heart is trembling like a willow
Desiring my cypress the pleasure of a kiss.

To buy my heart, no interest she will show—
I won't sell her hair for the world's bliss.

If ever Hafiz's heart is relieved from sorrow,
Such faithful servant, my friend shall miss.

INTERPRETATION

You are expecting some good news, and are very impatient to receive it. Often you are disappointed that you will never get it. But you will get it, when you go on trip, being out of your city for some time.

صبا اگر گذری افتدت بکشور دوست / بیار نفحه‌ای از گیسوی معنبر دوست

بجان او که بشکرانه جان برافشانم / اگر بسوی من آری پیامی از بر دوست

وگر چنانکه در آن حضرتت نباشد بار / من گدا و تمنای وصل او و هیهات

دل صنوبریم همچو بید لرزانست / ز حسرت قد و بالای چون صنوبر دوست

اگر چه دوست بچیزی نمیخرد ما را / بعالمی نفروشیم موئی از سر دوست

چه باشد ار شود از بند غم دلش آزاد
چو هست حافظ مسکین غلام و چاکر دوست

53

Enjoy good company in a garden at Spring,
What's the Saki waiting for: Where's she?

Make the most of your time, where'er you may be,
For no one knows what tomorrow will bring.

Lo! Your life is tied to a tender string.
Enjoy yourself and of worries be free.

The "life-water" and "Paradise-garden" to me,
Are: The wine at brookside and my darling.

The veiled and mellow beauties are of one origin.
Whose charm I ought to follow, you will say?

Even Heaven doesn't know the secrets within,
Why then with the curtain-holder quarrel you may?

If God won't forgive my trespass and sin
What means then, God's mercy for the astray?

Pious wish paradise, Hafiz the wine unclean;
What God wishes for us, will count, anyway.

INTERPRETATION

Not knowing what Fate has in store for us, we must all be happy and make the most of our time. We must not give chances to worries. You are now in a dilemma about two things that you want to do and do not know which one to do. Never mind, choose what you think best and rest assured that if you are sincere in your intentions, God will help you out, even if you make slight mistakes. Be sure God will assist you and you will get worldly success.

خوشتر ز عیش و صحبت و باغ و بهار چیست؟   ساقی کجاست گو سبب انتظار چیست؟

هر وقت خوش که دست دهد مغتنم شمار   کس را وقوف نیست که انجام کار چیست

پیوند عمر بسته به مویست هوش دار   غمخوار خویش باش غم روزگار چیست

معنی آب زندگی و روضهٔ ارم   جز طرف جویبار و می خوشگوار چیست

مستور و مست هر دو چو از یک قبیله‌اند   ما دل بشوهٔ که دهیم اختیار چیست

راز درون پرده چه داند فلک خموش   ای مدعی نزاع تو با پرده دار چیست

سهو و خطای بنده گرش اعتبار نیست   معنی عفو و رحمت آمرزگار چیست

زاهد شراب کوثر و حافظ پیاله خواست

تا در میانه خواسته کردگار چیست

O' Nightingale! Sympathise with me and cry;
Nothing better than this for lovers to try.

Serve wine! Our wine-smeared shamful cloak we deride.
The clergy isn't sober, being drunk with pride.

To the crude-in-love, your curls give no pain-
Libertines desire to be under such chain.

Pure love emanates from a source divine.
But not from ruby lips and figures fine.

Beauty isn't in eyes, curls, mole or the face;
Many secrets involved therein besides grace.

The satin robes of those who lack wisdom,
Is not worth a penny in truth's kingdom.

One can hardly gain access to you-
It's hard to ascend to the firmament blue.

Hafiz, don't bother her with moaning alarm,
Eternal bliss comes to those who do no harm.

INTERPRETATION

You may feel very melancholy for what has already happened. But never mind; what you are suffering from, seems to be suffered by most people. There is a sense of relief in this suffering for you and you like it in spite of hardships. People may think that because they have wealth, influence etc. , they will succeed, but this is not true in all cases, for often some tact, lenience and friendship may also be needed. Money, wealth and influence without due foresight and tact will not bring good results. What you are after, is very difficult to get but if you keep on acting with great tact and a spirit of friendship and a generous turn of mind, you will get what you desire, and when you get it, it will give you a great and lasting remuneration.

بنال بلبل اگر با منت سر یاریست   که ما دو عاشق زاریم و کار ما زاریست

در آن زمین که نسیمی وزد ز طره دوست   چه جای دم زدن نافهای تاتاریست

بیار باده که رنگین کنیم جامه زرق   که مست جام غروریم و نام هشیاریست

خیال زلف تو پختن نه کار هر خامیست   که زیر سلسله رفتن طریق عیاریست

لطیفه‌ایست نهانی که عشق ازو خیزد   که نام آن نه لب لعل و خط زنگاریست

جمال شخص نه چشم است و زلف و عارض و خال   هزار نکته در این کار و بار دلداریست

قلندران حقیقت به نیم جو نخرند   قبای اطلس آن کس که از هنر عاریست

بر آستان تو مشکل توان رسید آری   عروج بر فلک سروری به دشواریست

سحر کرشمه چشمت به خواب می‌دیدم   زهی مراتب خوابی که به ز بیداریست

دلش به ناله میازار و ختم کن حافظ

که رستگاری جاوید در کم آزاریست

The conceited pious, doesn't know my state.
Whatever he may say of me, I never mind.

In a direct path, your way you easily find.
Take what comes up and accept it as your fate.

Risk a pawn to avoid becoming checkmate,
Ne'er risk your king, e'en if your game's behind.

This high dome is simple, yet complexly designed,
No Sage ever knows, secrets behind the gate.

What's the secret, O' Lord, mighty and great,
So many sores exist, but no remedy of any kind.

The Master I'm sure isn't ignorant or blind-
No record he keeps of our love and hate.

God is not proud, has no porters I'm sure.
Come just as you are; He'll take us all!

I'm true to the Sage, for his love is pure,
Whereas the Sheikh's grace may rise and fall.

Hafiz has no seats in front rows secure-
Libertine-lovers care not what may befall.

INTERPRETATION

*Some people may misjudge you, but you being sure of your
sincerity of purpose, do not mind. If you are straightforward, you will
get what you want easily. You may take chances and make risks,
but never take great risks that may ruin your whole life. You may find
that you have many problems without solution, but never mind, for
God will help us in all our ways. You may not get to the highest rank
in your line, but since you will be happy and successful, this does not
matter.*

غزنیات حافظ

زاهد ظاهرپرست ازحال ما آگاه نیست / درحق ما هرچه گوید جای هیچ اکراه نیست

درطریقت هرچه پیش سالک آید خیر اوست / درصراط مستقیم ای دل کسی گمراه نیست

تاچه بازی رخ نماید بیدقی خواهیم راند / عرصه شطرنج رندان را مجال شاه نیست

چیست این سقف بلند ساده بسیار نقش / زین معما هیچ دانا درجهان آگاه نیست

این چه استغناست یارب وین چه قادر حکمت / کاین همه زخم نهان هست ومجال آه نیست

صاحب دیوان ما گویی نمی‌داند حساب / کاندرین طغرا نشان حسبه لله نیست

هرکه خواهد گو بیا وهرچه خواهد گو بگو / کبر ونازوحاجب ودربان بدین درگاه نیست

بردر میخانه رفتن کار یک‌رنگان بود / خودفروشان را به کوی می‌فروشان راه نیست

هرچه هست از قامت ناساز بی‌اندام ماست / ورنه تشریف تو بربالای کس کوتاه نیست

بنده پیر خراباتم که لطفش دائم است / ورنه لطف شیخ وزاهد گاه هست وگاه نیست

حافظ ار بر صدر ننشیند زعالی مشربیست / عاشق دردی‌کش اندربند مال وجاه نیست

59

No safety in love; It's a dangerous road;
No choice here but to put life at random.

To your heart,love must always be welcome,
Good deeds are welcome at home or abroad.

Wisdom bids me go to the wine abode,
Though wisdom has no say in my kingdom.

Your eyes are guilty for my martyrdom,
In a chariot of love towards destiny I rode.

My love-crescent,only keen eyes can see;
Weak eyes won't see my darling earthly moon

Drink and make the most of your opportunity,
For few know the value of this fortune.

The cries of Hafiz have no effect in thee!
Will your stone-heart pity my misfortune?

INTERPRETATION

What you have undertaken is a dangerous task, and you should know this well. But if you do good, wherever you are, you will be well rewarded. Only people of great insight can see what great opportunities lie before them. Meantime, never fail to be happy and spend your life with joy. Perhaps your great efforts will bring you good results in the end.

نير

راهیست راه عشق که هیچش کناره نیست
اینجا جز آنکه جان بسپارند چاره نیست

هر گه که دل به عشق دهی خوش دمی بود
در کار خیر حاجت هیچ استخاره نیست

ما را ز منع عقل مترسان و می بیار
کان شحنه در ولایت ما هیچ کاره نیست

از چشم خود بپرس که ما را که می‌کشد
جانا گناه طالع و جرم ستاره نیست

او را به چشم پاک توان دید چون هلال
هر دیده جای جلوهٔ آن ماه پاره نیست

فرصت شمر طریقهٔ رندی که این نشان
چون راه گنج بر همه کس آشکاره نیست

نگرفت در تو گریهٔ حافظ بهیچ رو
حیران آن دلم که کم از سنگ خاره نیست

61

A nightingale had a gay-colored rose on bill;
For partial success it sang with a sigh.

"You've the rose" I said, "what makes you cry?"
It said: "Love's charm put me to this thrill!"

No wonder she doesn't sit with me, nor will,
Being a thriving queen, to a beggar she's shy.

Her coquetry my devotion won't buy,
Blessed is he whose love-cup will fill.

The Painter did wonders with masterly pen,
Many masterpieces with His compasses he made.

If you follow love, fear no ignominy then,
The Sheikh pawned his robe and the tavern thus paid.

The running waters of paradise garden,
Remind Hafiz's tears at the abode of his maid.

INTERPRETATION

You will have a partial success in your career for which you will be happy and thrilled. You are a bit disappointed that you will not succeed in your plans, but if you do things with a spirit of love, do not fear anything. When you are successful, you will look back with surprise over your past worries and doubts.

بلبلی برگ گلی خوش رنگ در منقار داشت
و اندر آن برگ و نوا خوش ناله‌های زار داشت

گفتمش در عین وصل این ناله و فریاد چیست
گفت ما را جلوهٔ معشوق در این کار داشت

یار اگر ننشست با ما نیست جای اعتراض
پادشاهی کامران بود از گدایی عار داشت

در نگیرد ناز و نیاز ما به حسن دوست
خرم آن کز نازنینان بخت برخوردار داشت

خیز تا بر کلک آن نقاش جان افشان کنیم
کاین همه نقش عجب در گردش پرگار داشت

گر مریدِ راه عشقی فکر بدنامی مکن
شیخ صنعان خرقه رهن خانهٔ خمار داشت

وقت آن شیرین قلندر خوش که در اطوار سیر
ذکرِ تسبیح ملک در حلقهٔ زنار داشت

چشم حافظ زیر بام قصر آن حوری سرشت
شیوهٔ جنات تجری تحتها الانهار داشت

The refreshing wine and charming beauties I enjoy,
Now that the garden spreads a fragrant breeze.

Any beggar can now a kingdom of riches seize-
Green fields my garden, rainy clouds my joy.

The turf tells the story of April-love, O'boy,
Don't spoil present comfort for future ease.

Enjoy your love and thus your soul appease—
With our mud the world bricks 'll make 'n' destroy.

From your friend no loyalty you will gain,
A monastery candle won't do for altar fire.

Don't blame me for breaking repentance again,
Who knows what destiny will require?

Follow Hafiz's corpse to the grave with pain,
For though sinful, paradise he will acquire.

INTERPRETATION

There is a chance of great success for you now, and, you should take advantage of it at once. Many people can now get great benefits. Don't spoil your pleasant joys for future comfort. Don't expect too much from your present chances. Although you had shortcomings, you will gain the paradise of success.

من و شراب فرح‌بخش و یار حورسرشت   کنون که می‌دمد از بوستان نسیم بهشت

که خیمه سایهٔ ابرست و بزمگاه کشت   گدا چرا نزند لاف سلطنت امروز

نه عاقل است که نسیه خرید و نقد بهشت   چمن حکایت اردی‌بهشت می‌گوید

بر آن سرست که از خاک ما بسازد خشت   به می عمارت دل کن که این جهان خراب

چو شمع صومعه افروزی از چراغ کنشت   وفا مجوی ز دشمن که پرتوی ندهد

که آگه است که تقدیر بر سرش چه نوشت   مکن به نامه سیاهی ملامت من مست

قدم دریغ مدار از جنازهٔ حافظ

که گرچه غرق گناه است می‌رود به بهشت

Pious clergy! Don't mind libertines like me,
For you won't account for other people's sin.

Mind your business, why in others you're keen?
What we sow today, its fruit tomorrow see.

The sober and drunk,lovers desire to be.
In mosque or altar, the dominant love is seen.

I bow before tavern door; it is clean.
Enemies may break my neck, they are free.

Don't give up hope of God's eternal grace.
You don't know before God who is bad or fine.

I am not alone who impiety embrace,
My father Adam, gave up paradise divine!

Hafiz, after tavern, paradise is your place,
Provided at death you get a cup of wine.

INTERPRETATION

People may criticise you but don't pay any attention to them. Be hopeful for efforts of today, as they will bring results tomorrow. In spite of the opposition of certain people, you are steadfast in your action. Don't be disappointed of God's grace, for He will favor you with His blessings. Cheer up, for your unhappy days will end into happiness and success.

عیب رندان مکن ای زاهد پاکیزه سرشت
که گناه دگران بر تو نخواهند نوشت

من اگر نیکم و گر بد تو برو خود را باش
هر کسی آن درود عاقبت کار که کشت

همه کس طالب یارند چه هشیار و چه مست
همه جا خانهٔ عشق است چه مسجد چه کنشت

سر تسلیم من و خشت در میکده ها
مدعی گر نکند فهم سخن گو سر و خشت

ناامیدم مکن از سابقهٔ لطف ازل
تو پس پرده چه دانی که که خوبست و که زشت

نه من از پردهٔ تقوی بدر افتادم و بس
پدرم نیز بهشت ابد از دست بهشت

حافظا روز اجل گر بکف آری جامی
یکسر از کوی خرابات برندت به بهشت

67

The world 's captured by your beauty and grace.
With unity you capture the world and space.

The candle, divulging secrets of the friend,
Was burned by the tongue and its life came to end.

Of the hidden fire of love inside my chest,
The glowing sun is the simile best.

The rose desiring to imitate her color and scent,
Was reproached by Zephyr and forced to repent.

Saki's image reflected in the cup by fire,
Justified me the wine-cup to admire.

Drink, for those who know what comes up,
Lighted from sorrow, by taking heavy cup.

With anemone blood is written on the rose,
"Only men of experience, purple wine chose."

Hafiz, since grace drips from your pen,
How can the jealous, find fault with you then?

INTERPRETATION

*If you unite your efforts with other friends, you can do wonders.
Keep your secrets; otherwise you will pay dearly for it. There is a
glowing light of ambition inside you. Since you are so graceful and
kind, no one can harm you.*

حسنت بانفاق صلاحت جهان گرفت / آری بانفاق جهان می توان گرفت

افشای راز خلوتیان خواست کرد شمع / شکر خدا که سرّ دلش در زبان گرفت

زین آتش نهفته که در سینه من است / خورشید شعله ایست که در آسمان گرفت

می خواست گل که دم زند از رنگ و بوی دوست / از غیرت صبا نفسش در دهان گرفت

آسوده بر کنار چو پرگار می شدم / دوران چو نقطه عاقبتم در میان گرفت

آن روز شوق ساغر می خرمنم بسوخت / کاتش ز عکس عارض ساقی در آن گرفت

خواهم شدن بکوی مغان آستین فشان / زین فتنه ها که دامن آخر زمان گرفت

می خور که هر که آخر کار جهان بدید / از غم سبک برآمد و رطل گران گرفت

بر برگ گل بخون شقایق نوشته اند / کانکس که پخته شد می چون ارغوان گرفت

حافظ چو آب لطف ز نظم تو می چکد / حاسد چگونه نکته تواند بر آن گرفت

The Sage's advice, in my memory 'll remain;-
"Agonies of separation you can never explain."

The preacher telling tortures of resurrection,
Was only referring to the friend's separation.

Whom can I ask about my wandering friend;
What Zephyr tells in distress, can't comprehend.

Alas! my love-ignoring friend isn't kind!
How easily about friends she changes her mind!

I'm still content, though rivals will thank;
My heart's used to pain; let me be frank.

Remedy your old troubles with the old wine;
"Wine brings you joy" said the Sage divine.

This was Zephyr's advice, to King Solomon indeed;-
"Don't tie knots on wind, for you won't succeed."

The few-days' life shouldn't lead you astray;
This cunning old hag, never changes her way.

Take things easy, for the fortunate man
To please his friend will do what he can.

Who said "Hafiz forgot his sweetheart"?
From such sweet beauty, I'd never depart.

INTERPRETATION

You are going on a rather long journey soon. Some of your friends may forget you for a while. But what you should remember is that you should not cherish wild and impractical hopes, for in that case you will not succeed. Remember that life means strife and toil, and so cheer up with happy pursuits of life. Take things easy and rest assured that God will never forsake you.

70

شنیده‌ام سخنی خوش که پیر کنعان گفت / فراق یار نه آن می‌کند که بتوان گفت

حدیث هول قیامت که گفت واعظ شهر / کنایتیست که از روزگار هجران گفت

نشان یار سفر کرده از که پرسم باز / که هرچه گفت برید صبا پریشان گفت

فغان که آن مه نامهربان مهر گسل / بترک صحبت یاران خود چه آسان گفت

من و مقام رضا بعد ازین و شکر رقیب / که دل بدرد تو خو کرد و ترک درمان گفت

غم کهن به می سالخورده دفع کنید / که تخم خوشدلی اینست پیر دهقان گفت

گره به باد مزن گرچه بر مراد رود / که این سخن به مثل باد با سلیمان گفت

بمعصیت که سپهرت بهر زراه مرو / تراکه گفت که این آل ترکستان گفت

مزن ز چون و چرا دم که بنده مقبل / قبول کرد بجان هر سخن که جانان گفت

که گفت حافظ از اندیشه تو آمد باز / من این نگفته‌ام آنکس که گفت بهتان گفت

If your religion, the blood of lovers demands;
Just say so, and I'll obey your commands.

Your dark hair accounts for darkness of the night;
Your bright face explains why morning 's bright.

No one can escape from her curls' lasso;
Nor darts of her looks or bow of eyebrow.

A spring of tears I shed because of your whim,
In this spring no sailor dares to swim.

Your life-giving lips when my lips met,
Life and energy from them did sure get.

After many requests your lips gave a kiss;
Many sacrifices I made to get this bliss.

All your lovers pray for your joy and delight,
To live as long as there is day and night.

Expedience or piety Hafiz never had;
No one expects these things from a lover mad.

INTERPRETATION

Your dark days will end into bright ones. You have suffered much in the way of love, or in the way of your career. But soon you will face success and get what you want. The sacrifices you made are well worth for what you get. You will enjoy a prolonged happiness and success.

اگر بذهب تو خون عاشق مشب مباح
صلاح ما همه آنست کان ترا صلاح

سواد زلف سیاه تو جامل الظلمات
بیاض روی چو ماه تو فاتق الاصباح

زمین زانگ کندت کنی نباقت خلاص
از آن کا پنجه ابر و تیر مژه نجاح

زدیده ام شده و یک چشمه در کنار روان
لب چو آب حیات تو هست تشنه جان

بداد لعل لبت بوسه بصد زاری
گرفت کام و دلم زو بصد هزار لکاح

دعای جان تو ورد زبان تشنه گانست
همیشه تا که بود وقت شام و مساوصباح

صلاح و توبه و تقوی ز ماجمو حافظ
زرند و عاشق و مجنون کسی نباقت صلاح

Plant herb of friendship; it brings success.
Uproot tree of enmity; it causes distress.

While at the tavern behave with respect;
From wine toxity hangover you may expect.

Enjoy her nocturnal company, for you die in sin;
And many nights and days this world 'll spin.

Bring a palfrey for Leily, pride of the Moon-
Perhaps God'll guide her pass by this Majnoon

Seek with all your might the life spring;
For jonquils 'n' nightingales turf 'll bring.

With her curls my heart made a covenant pure;
Her sweet lips my comfort will secure.

Hafiz! By cypress beauties at turf sit still;
Never mind if it's your will or God's will.

INTERPRETATION

Try to befriend everybody and avoid hatred and enmity. Your success depends on winning friends and reducing the number of your enemies. There is a good chance that you will gain success. Seek happiness and spend your time in the best way, for your means of happiness are all ready. Soon you will get what you are after, and this will bring you great comfort and security.

درخت دوستی بنشان که کام دل ببار آرد
نهال دشمنی برکن که رنج بی شمار آرد

چو مهمان خراباتی بعزت باش با رندان
که در سرکشی جان اگرت مستی خمار آرد

شب صحبت غنیمت دان که بعد از روزگار ما
بسی گردش کند گردون بسی لیل و نهار آرد

عماری دار لیلی را که مهد ماه در حکمست
خدا را در دل اندازش که بر مجنون گذار آرد

بهار عمر خواه ای دل و گرنه این چمن هر سال
چو نسرین صد گل آرد بار و چون بلبل هزار آرد

خدا را چون دل ریشم قراری بست با زلفت
بفرما لعل نوشین را که زودش با قرار آرد

درین باغ از خدا خواهد دگر پیرانه سر حافظ
نشیند بر لب جوئی و سروی در کنار آرد

If with godly men friendship you make,
God 'll assist you in whatever you undertake.

The friend's story but to him must be told;
For friends' secrets only friends can hold.

O'heart! Live pure, for if your feet slide
Angels with uplifted hands near you abide.

If from your lover loyalty you claim;
Be loyal to her, for she'll do the same.

I told her: "Let my heart with you go."
"I can't help it" she said, "Let God do so."

My heart! Your body and soul give to the friend
Who observes loyalty to the very end.

Help Hafiz find the dust of her road,
To keep as a souvenir in my abode.

INTERPRETATION

If you have godly friends, God will assist you to succeed in your efforts. Be careful not to divulge secrets and keep your tongue tightly closed. If you live purely and without fatal mistakes, you will be protected by a mysterious hand. If you seek loyalty, be loyal yourself. You are now making every effort to get what you want, but if you are loyal, you will get it.

هر آنکه جانب اهل خدا نگه دارد   خداش در همه حال از بلا نگه دارد

حدیث دوست نگویم مگر بحضر دوست   که آشنا سخن آشنا نگه دارد

دلا معاش چنان کن که گر بلغزد پای   فرشته‌ات به دو دست دعا نگه دارد

گرت هواست که معشوق نگسلد پیمان   نگاه دار سررشته تا نگه دارد

صبا بر آن سر زلف ار دل مرا بینی   ز روی لطف بگویش که جا نگه دارد

چو گفتمش که دلم را نگاه دار چه گفت   ز دست بنده چه خیزد خدا نگه دارد

سر و زر و دل و جانم فدای آن یاری   که حق صحبت مهر و وفا نگه دارد

غبار راه گذارت کجاست تا حافظ
بیادگار نسیم صبا نگه دارد

A lovely tune played the musician of love,
The tunes played, came from Heaven above.

The world is never free from lovers' groan,
Though the tune of love is a melancholy moan.

Though wine-seller Sage, has no gold to give;
His merciful God his sins will forgive.

Cherish my heart, for it is a lover true;
My heart is exalted when I think of you.

It is only fair if sometimes a king,
To his poor neighbor favor may bring.

I showed bleeding tears to doctor, said he :-
"The love-disease has a heart-rending remedy."

The tyranny of your oglings you better forget,
In kingdom of love, rewards for deeds you get.

How well said Saki — beautiful and slim :
"Worship the face that has truth in him."

O' queen! at your threshold Hafiz shall pray,
In response he expects you a kind word to say.

INTERPRETATION

You will have a golden chance at your disposal. You will get this without spending much money or efforts. It will be a great privilege brought to you and bestowed upon you by people of great prestige and importance.

مطرب عشق عجب ساز و نوائی دارد / نقش هر نغمه که زد راه بجائی دارد

عالم از ناله عشاق مبادا خالی / که خوش آهنگ و فرح بخش هوائی دارد

پیر دردی کش ما گرچه ندارد زر و زور / خوش عطا بخش و خطا پوش خدائی دارد

محترم دار دلم کاین مگس قندپرست / تا هوا خواه تو شد فره همائی دارد

از عدالت نبود دور گرش پرسد حال / پادشاهی که بهمسایه گدائی دارد

اشک خونین بنمودم بطبیبان گفتند / درد عشقست و جگر سوز دوائی دارد

ستم از غمزه میاموز که در مذهب عشق / هر عمل اجری و هر کرده جزائی دارد

نغز گفت آن بت ترسا بچه باده پرست / شادی روی کسی خور که صفائی دارد

خسروا حافظ درگاه نشین فاتحه خواند / وز زبان تو تمنای دعائی دارد

Without the friend I have no interest in life.
My life without Him is agony and strife.

No sign of God! How can I,HIM define?
Either I know not, or He has no sign.

The home of security one can't give up.
It's endless road; O' caravan guide, stop.

Stooping lyre calls you to happiness and joy,
Listen to what old lyre says, O'Young Boy!

"Learn from the Sheriff– that cunning fellow–
"Though heavily drunk, no one thinks him mellow."

"Croesus and his treasures, plundered by Time;
"Don't hide your gold" Harp played this rhyme.

Tell no secrets to your enemy; it's wrong;
For even headless candle can't keep its tongue.

Hafiz is a servant unparalleled and true.
He has a master who is unparalleled too.

INTERPRETATION

In all your activities, you should observe the safety rules and do not run unnecessary risks. You have to be a little more careful in your future activities. Sometimes you show yourself, before the people, much worse than you really are, which should be avoided. Do not store up your money, but spend as you get. Trust no one and keep your secrets with you. If you do these, you will be much respected by your superiors, and they will consider you as an exceptional person.

جان بی جمال جانان میل جهان ندارد   هر کس که این ندارد حقا که آن ندارد

با هیچ کس نشانی زان دلستان ندیدم   یا من خبر ندارم یا او نشان ندارد

هر شبنمی درین ره صد بحر آتشینست   دردا که این معما شرح و بیان ندارد

سر منزل فراغت نتوان ز دست دادن   ای ساروان فرو کش کاین ره کران ندارد

چنگ خمیده قامت میخواندت به عشرت   بشنو که پند پیران هیچت زیان ندارد

ای دل طریق رندی از محتسب بیاموز   مست است و در حق او کس این گمان ندارد

احوال گنج قارون کایام داد بر باد   در گوش دل فرو خوان تا زر نهان ندارد

گر خود رقیب شمع است اسرار از او بپوشان   کان شوخ سر بریده بند زبان ندارد

کس در جهان ندارد یک بنده همچو حافظ

زیرا که چون تو شاهی کس در جهان ندارد

The glow of your face, the moon doesn't possess,
The rose before you is withered leaf I guess.

Your eyebrows are the resting place of my soul,
The king can't seek a better altar as his goal.

Look! Impertinent narcissus opened up before you!
It was impolite. Such a thing it shouldn't do.

I will suffer pain since her heart is shy,
And can't suffer to hear complainant's cry.

If to her threshold you can't find your way,
With the blood of liver your sleeves wash away.

I am not alone plundered by her curl;
Many are plundered by my black-haired girl.

If Hafiz worships you, no objection bring,
One profane to love, isn't guilty of anything.

INTERPRETATION

*You will get such great success that few people will outshine you.
Many people will turn to you for solution of their problems. No one
will dare oppose you or compete with you. Meantime try to be fair to
all, and do not get mad with people for their mistakes or trespasses.*

روشنی طلعت تو ماه ندارد   پیش تو گل رونق گیاه ندارد

گوشهٔ ابروی تست منزل جانم   خوشتر ازین گوشه پادشاه ندارد

تا چه کند با رخ تو دود دل من   آینه دانی که تاب آه ندارد

شوخی نرگس نگر که پیش تو بشکفت   چشم دریده ادب نگاه ندارد

دیدم و آن چشم دل سیه که تو داری   جانب هیچ آشنا نگاه ندارد

رطل گرانم ده ای مرید خرابات   شادی شیخی که خانقاه ندارد

خون خور و خامش نشین که آن دل نازک   طاقت فریاد دادخواه ندارد

گو برو و آستین بخون جگر شوی   هر که درین آستانه راه ندارد

فی من تنها کشم تطاول زلفت   کیست که او داغ آن سیاه ندارد

حافظ اگر سجده تو کرد مکن عیب

کافر عشق ای صنم گناه ندارد

With much heart - blood, a nightingale got a rose,
But the angry wind caused the thorns to oppose.

A parrot dreaming of sugar, was really gay,
When the flood of death, carried it away.

I wish the friend would understand my strife.
She came easy, but difficult made my life!

O cameleer, for God's sake, help me on
The hope of help led me to this caravan.

Don't ignore my wet eyes and dusty face,
Therein the blue dome made its home of grace.

Alas! the jealous moon of the blue sky,
Will cause my earthly moon in grave to lie.

Hafiz, you die and can't enjoy her face;
The Time's foul play deprived you of her grace.

INTERPRETATION

You will make success with great strife, but there will be much opposition against you. However, this success will not take long. It will be an easy success, but will make things difficult for you later on. You are expecting help from some source now, but do not forget that your strife and toil will bring you further blessings. It will honor you with many privileges. But even these privileges won't last long, and through jealousy and oppositions, they will be taken away.

بلبلی خون دلی خورد و گلی حاصل کرد با د غیرت بصد تش خار پریشان دل کرد

طوطیی را به خیال شکری دل خوش بود نا گهش سیل فنا نقش امل باطل کرد

قرة العین من آن میوهٔ دل یادش باد که چه آسان بشد و کارمرا مشکل کرد

ساروان بار من افتاد خدا را مددی که امید کرم همره این محمل کرد

روی خاکی و نم چشم مرا خوارمدار چرخ فیروزه طربخانه ازین کهگل کرد

آه و فریاد که از چشم حسود مه چرخ در لحد ماه کمان ابروی من منزل کرد

نزدی شاه رخ و فوت شد امکان حافظ
چکنم بازی ایام مرا غافل کرد

As Zephyr I fly to the mansion of the friend,
My breath with her sweet scent I will blend.

No life without the friend, the wine and rhyme,
No more can I endure this waste of time.

All the credit for wisdom and piety I get,
Will bargain for the dust of her road, I bet.

My life candle is by God's love aglow;
My whole life at God's threshold I throw.

In memory of her eyes, myself destroy,
Thus fulfill my old covenant to my joy.

O' Zephyr, my bleeding heart, like the rose,
To friend's fragrance as ransom I expose.

Hafiz, hatred and sham remove the peace of heart,
The libertine-love I chose to be my part.

INTERPRETATION

You will soon make a trip and enjoy a good pleasure. You are willing to sacrifice everything for the success you expect to get. But meantime, you are a religious man, devoted to God, and ready to make any sacrifices for Him. You are a true lover of God, no matter what people may say of you.

86

چو با دعزم سر کوی یار خواهم کرد   نفس بوی خوشش مشکبار خواهم کرد

بهرزه بی می و معشوق عمر میگذرد   بطلا نسم بس از امروز کار خواهم کرد

هر آب رویی که اندوختم ز دانش و دین   نثار خاک ره آن نگار خواهم کرد

چو شمع صبحدم شد ز مهر او روشن   که عمر در سر این کار بار خواهم کرد

بیا و چشم تو خود در اخراب اهم خست   بنای عهد قدیم استوار خواهم کرد

صبا کجاست که این جان خون گرفته چو گل   فدای نکهت گیسوی یار خواهم کرد

نفاق و زرق نبخشد صفای دل حافظ
طریق رندی و مشق اختیار خواهم کرد

87

One cannot touch her ringlets twofold,
Or rely on Zephyr, nor on what she told.

For reaching you I'd do whatever I can,
But man cannot change destiny's plan.

With a bleeding heart her skirt I approach,
I wouldn't easily let go, though enemies reproach.

Her face was resembled to the moon of the sky,
It isn't good simile though the moon is high.

A clear vision can really, her face see,
In a mirror one looks as one should be.

The riddle of love is beyond man's wisdom;
This is not solved in man's mortal kingdom.

I'm jealous that she 's loved by everyone;
But can't beat everyone being all alone.

What to say when you 're so tender and vigil,
That even my prayers, your peace disturb will !

Towards your eyebrow I worship all the time,
To worship another, in my faith is a crime.

INTERPRETATION

Do not depend on promises given to you by certain friends. You will stick fast to your aim and will not falter even if everybody reproaches you. Don't feel bad because the one you love is liked by everybody— being beautiful and charming. You are consistent in your plans and that will lead you to success.

دست در حلقهٔ آن زلف دوتا نتوان کرد   تکیه بر عهد تو و باد صبا نتوان کرد

آنچه سعی است من اندر طلبت بنمایم   این قدر هست که تغییر قضا نتوان کرد

دامن دوست به صد خون دل افتاد به دست   به فسوسی که کند خصم رها نتوان کرد

عارضش را به مثل ماه فلک نتوان گفت   نسبت دوست به هر بی سر و پا نتوان کرد

سرو بالای من آنگه که درآید به سماع   چه محل جامهٔ جان را که قبا نتوان کرد

نظر پاک تواند رخ جانان دیدن   که در آیینه نظر جز به صفا نتوان کرد

مشکل عشق نه در حوصلهٔ دانش ماست   حل این نکته بدین فکر خطا نتوان کرد

غیرتم کشت که محبوب جهانی لیکن   روز و شب عربده با خلق خدا نتوان کرد

من چه گویم که ترا نازکی طبع لطیف   تا به حدیست که آهسته دعا نتوان کرد

بجز ابروی تو محراب دل حافظ نیست

طاعت غیر تو در مذهب ما نتوان کرد

My darling went—a word to lovers didn't send—
She has forgotten her old travelling friend.

Either my luck has never loyalty witnessed,
Or she never in life loyalty expressed.

I thought I could soften her heart with tears,
But her heart is hard as stone, it appears.

The impatient bird of my sad heart I bet,
The dream of her love-snare will never forget.

Those who saw her beauty my eyes never blame,
For my eyes with forethought selected its aim.

Burning as candle, Hafiz gives his soul,
Like the dawn-breeze, she won't my heart console.

INTERPRETATION

You may not hear news from your friend for some time, and feel very unhappy about it. You are happy with the recollection of the past days of fun you have had. You are very impatient to meet him or her again, but it will take some time before this dream comes true.

دلبر برفت و دلشدگان را خبر نکرد

یاد حریف شهر و رفیق سفر نکرد

یا بخت من طریق مروت فروگذاشت

یا او به شاهراه طریقت گذر نکرد

گفتم مگر به گریه دلش مهربان کنم

چون سخت بود در دل سنگش اثر نکرد

شوخی مکن که مرغ دل بیقرار من

سودای دام عاشقی از سر بدر نکرد

هر کس که دید روی تو بوسید چشم من

کاری که کرد دیده من بی نظر نکرد

من ایستاده تا کنمش جان فدا چو شمع

او خود گذر به ما چو نسیم سحر نکرد

My heart for years asked me Jam's cup to bring,
A stranger was asked, though itself possessed the thing.

This jewel that 's beyond all time and space,
My heart demanded, of what I have no trace.

I took this problem to my Sage by chance,
Since he unfolded secrets by a mere glance.

He was full 'o' joy,with the wine-cup in hand–
In that mirror reflected many a kingdom and land.

I asked: «When wisdom gave this crystal cup? »
He said : « When the Blue Dome,God had put up.»

A heartless, though with God, Him didn't see,
And cried from afar « Where art thee? »

"The friend who was crucified," said he,
"Was incriminated,since God he claimed to be"

If again the Holy Ghost souls would reform,
What was done by Christ, others can perform.

I asked "Why my beauty's curl is a chain?"
He said : "Hafiz, of enchained heart you complain."

INTERPRETATION

*You are asking other people to give you what already you possess.
Look well in yourself and you will see that you have what you already
seek. All that you want is with you and near you. Don't go too far.
If you get a little of the spiritual insight and strength,you will be able
to perform wonders. You may complain of your present entanglements
and difficulties, but be sure all these are worth for what you expect to
get.*

سالها دل طلب جام جم از ما میکرد
وانچه خود داشت ز بیگانه تمنا میکرد

گوهری کز صدف کون و مکان بیرون بود
طلب از گم شدگان لب دریا میکرد

مشکل خویش بر پیر مغان بردم دوش
کو به تأیید نظر حل معما میکرد

دیدمش خرم و خندان قدح باده بدست
و اندر آن آینه صد گونه تماشا میکرد

گفتم این جام جهان بین تو کی داد حکیم
گفت آنروز که این گنبد مینا میکرد

بیدلی در همه احوال خدا با او بود
او نمیدیدش و از دور خدا را میکرد

این همه شعبده خویش که میکرد اینجا
سامری پیش عصا و ید بیضا میکرد

گفت آن یار کزو گشت سر دار بلند
جرمش این بود که اسرار هویدا میکرد

فیض روح القدس ار باز مدد فرماید
دیگران هم بکنند آنچه مسیحا میکرد

گفتمش سلسلهٔ زلف بتان از پی چیست
گفت حافظ گله ای از دل شیدا میکرد

Only when tavern-dust collyrium to your eyes make,
A glance at mysteries of Jam's cup you take.

Have music and wine in this earthly hell,
For only thus your sorrows you can dispel.

If true to the cause of love you always remain,
Many benefits you gain from this bargain.

So long as in the domain of flesh you stay,
To the house of truth you will find no way.

The friend has no cover, nor veil on face,
Shake off sham's dust, if you seek his grace.

So long as the cup and her lips you desire,
Nothing else in this world you will aspire.

O Heart! If only the light of truth you know,
Laughing like candle you will burn aglow.

Hafiz, this timely advice, better obey :
To the road of truth, you find your way.

INTERPRETATION

Only when you appreciate the great blessings around you, you will be able to unfold the secrets of this world. Never waste your time in useless worries and sorrows, but spend your time in happiness, for this happiness gives you a chance to think better and solve your problems. In order to see spiritual things, you must have spiritual vision. You seem to have concentrated all your efforts now on what you want to get. If you be a little more truthful and suffer a little more self-sacrifice, you will find your way to it.

94

غزلیات حافظ

به سر جام جم آنگه نظر توانی کرد
که خاک میکده کحل بصر توانی کرد

مباش بی می و مطرب که زیر طاق سپهر
بدین ترانه غم از دل بدر توانی کرد

گل مراد تو آنگه نقاب بگشاید
که خدمتش چو نسیم سحر توانی کرد

گدائی در میخانه طرفه اکسیریست
گر این عمل بکنی خاک زر توانی کرد

بعزم مرحلهٔ عشق پیش نه قدمی
که سودها کنی ار این سفر توانی کرد

تو کز سرای طبیعت نمیروی بیرون
کجا بکوی طریقت گذر توانی کرد

جمال یار ندارد نقاب و پرده ولی
غبار ره بنشان تا نظر توانی کرد

بیا که چارهٔ ذوق حضور و نظم امور
بفیض بخشی اهل نظر توانی کرد

ولی تو تا لب معشوق و جام می خواهی
طمع مدار که کار دگر توانی کرد

دلا ز نور هدایت گر آگهی یابی
چو شمع خنده زنان ترک سر توانی کرد

گر این نصیحت شاهانه بشنوی حافظ
بشاهراه حقیقت گذر توانی کرد

Only the beauties' love, my heart'll accept,
For anything but love, I have no concept.

O' Counsellor, speak of love and its bliss,
For in my opinion, nothing 's better than this.

O' Rose-faced Saki, that rosy wine bring!
Happiness doesn't come from any other thing.

I hide the cup-people a book may think.
No wonder, indeed, colorless is hypocricy's ink.

This ragged cloak, I'm going to burn up,
Since the Sage doesn't take in lieu of a cup.

Nothing but truth her ruby lips reveal,
To men of truth, then it has no appeal.

Don't ask me to forget such face and eyes,
If I obey your advice, I'm not wise.

Your enchanting eyes, so cunning and smart,
Though wild as wild birds, have hunted my heart.

O' wealthy man, remember the Dervish today,
For he goes nowhere else; knows no other way.

Hafiz, your sweet poetry is well told:
The king will shower you with riches and gold.

INTERPRETATION

At the age you are, you may seem to put too much emphasis on love and beauty. You may think that this is the only thing that brings you happiness. Before other people you may try to hide your love and pleasure. But remember that always the truth will prevail. Be truthful and do good to those needing your good deeds. God will help you.

دلم جز مهر مه رویان طریقی بر نمی‌گیرد   ز هر در می‌دهم پندش ولیکن در نمی‌گیرد

خدا را ای نصیحت گو حدیث ساغر و می گو   که نقشی در خیال ما از این خوشتر نمی‌گیرد

بیا ای ساقی گلرخ بیار و باده رنگین   که فکری در درون ما از این بهتر نمی‌گیرد

صراحی می‌کشم پنهان و مردم دفتر انگارند   عجب گر آتش این زرق در دفتر نمی‌گیرد

من این دلق مرقع را بخواهم سوختن روزی   که پیر می فروشانش بجامی بر نمی‌گیرد

از آن رو هست یاران را صفاها با می لعلش   که غیر از راستی نقشی در آن جوهر نمی‌گیرد

سر و چشمی چنین دلکش تو گویی چشم ازو بردوز   برو کاین وعظ بی معنی مرا در سر نمی‌گیرد

نصیحت گوی رندان را که با حکم قضا جنگست   دلش بس تنگ می‌بینم مگر ساغر نمی‌گیرد

چه خوش صید دلم کردی بنازم چشم مستت را   که کس مرغان وحشی را از این خوشتر نمی‌گیرد

خدا را رحمی ای منعم که درویش سر کویت   دری دیگر نمی‌داند رهی دیگر نمی‌گیرد

بدین شعر تر شیرین ز شاهنشه عجب دارم   که سر تا پای حافظ را چرا در زر نمی‌گیرد

If the Saki keeps serving wine this way,
All pious men drink wine all the day,.

If with her locks thus she covers her mole,
Many wisdom birds would fall in her chin-hole.

Happy is the drunk who at her feet may fall;
Sacrificing his head, his body and all.

The crude Zahid is loyal to wine by chance;
But mature wine inexperience will enhance.

Get wisdom in daytime—no time for drink—
Drinking in daytime, obscures the mind, I think.

The best time for the bright wine to enjoy,
Is when the dark night appears, my dear boy!

Never drink wine with the Sheriff, I say;
He drinks your wine and your cup takes away!

If Hafiz's luck gets his moon in the end,
To the Sun's corona joyfully he'd ascend.

INTERPRETATION

If you succeed the way you are now succeeding, many people will imitate you and do what you are doing. The benefits gained by you, will encourage many people to follow in your footsteps. It is indeed worth for you and all others to risk everything and to put things at stake, for the results are wonderful. Even those who try this occasionally, will find it beneficial. Spend your days in hard work and your nights in rest and happiness. Don't trust some of the high officials around you who may enjoy the conveniences put at their disposal by you while trying to create obstacles for you.

Cheer up, for in the end you will get a very outstanding success, which will make you the leading personality in your own line of activities.

ساقی ارباده ازین دست بجام انداز   عارفان را همه در شرب مدام انداز

وزچنین زیر خم زلف نهد دنبال   ای بسا مرغ خرد را که بدام انداز

ای خوشا دولت آن مست که در پای حریف   سرو دستار نداند که کدام انداز

زاهد خام که انکار می و جام کند   پخته گردد چو نظر بر می خام انداز

روز در کسب هنر کوش که می خوردن روز   دل چو در کسب آیینه در زنگ ظلام انداز

آنزمان وقت می صبح فروغست که شب   گرد خرگه که افق پرده شام انداز

باده با محتسب شهر ننوشی زنهار   بخورد بادهات و سنگ بجام انداز

حافظا ارز کله گوشه خورشید برآر

بخت ارقرعه بدان ماه تمام انداز

The world isn't worth spending a moment sad;
Sold my cloak for wine — this was all I had!

My cloak they didn't take at the tavern for a cup,
Such cloak of impiety why should I pick up!?

My opponent scornfully said, "Keep away" ;
"Your head isn't worth this door," he meant to say.

If you lose your head but gain a kingdom,
It's a silly bargain, far from wisdom.

The sea-dive seems easy with the hope of gain;
But the pearl isn't worth the storm and pain.

O Friend! Avoid lovers; keep' em in suspense;
A host of lovers you can never recompense.

Hafiz, give up the mean world and its conquest,
Gold is not worth from the mean to request.

INTERPRETATION

Spend everything you have for your happiness and comfort. Your opponents may ask you to give up your career because they may think you do not have the consistency to follow the case up. You should be very careful not to risk too much so that all chances of withdrawal may be ruined. At first glance you may think your enterprise is very easy and it will bring you lots of profit; but though you will succeed, yet the result will not be worth the effort and risk run into. Avoid numerous requests and stick to one of them, so that you can succeed; otherwise if you work in many directions the chances are remote for you. You may find in the long run that what you get will not be commensurate with your efforts.

می با غم بسر بردن جهان یکسر نمی‌ارزد   بی بغرو دوش و قی ما کزین بهتر نمی‌ارزد

بگوی می فروشانش بجایی برنمیگیرند   زهی سجاده ی تقوی که یک ساغر نمی‌ارزد

رقیبم سرزنشها کرد کزین باب رخ برتاب   چه افتاد این سرما را که خاک در نمی‌ارزد

شکوه ی تاج سلطانی که بیم جان در و درجست   کلاهی دلکش است اما به ترک سر نمی‌ارزد

چه آسان می‌نمود اول غم دریا ببوی سود   غلط کردم که این طوفان به صد گوهر نمی‌ارزد

ترا آن به که روی خود ز مشتاقان بپوشانی   که شادی جهانگیری غم لشکر نمی‌ارزد

چو حافظ در قناعت کوش و از دنیی دون بگذر
که یک جو منت دونان دو صد من زر نمی‌ارزد

At eternity rays of God's beauty did transpire,
Love appeared and put all existence to fire.

Later God sent Adam his glowing zeal,
For to the angel God's love did not appeal.

Wisdom desired some light from God's torch,
But was scolded by God's compassionate scorch.

A stranger desired God's secrecy with zest,
But a hidden hand hit him angrily on the chest.

All humans had their share of pleasure and fun,
My sore heart remained in misery alone.

Her chin's apple my lofty soul desires,
Though entrapped in her locks, her beauty admires.

Hafiz, only when happiness broke its pen,
Your love-story was to be written then.

INTERPRETATION

Love is the beginning of creation. Love is stronger than wisdom or anything else. What you now do is based on love and not on wisdom. If other persons try to interfere with your love, they will be defeated. You may think that all other human beings are happy except you, but this is not so. It is true, though, that in your efforts you will face lots of difficulties and often you will think that you are the only one faced with so great troubles.

در ازل پرتو حسنت ز تجلی دم زد
عشق پیدا شد و آتش به همه عالم زد

جلوه‌ای کرد رخت دید ملک عشق نداشت
عین آتش شد از این غیرت و بر آدم زد

عقل می‌خواست کز آن شعله چراغ افروزد
برق غیرت بدرخشید و جهان را هم زد

مدعی خواست که آید به تماشاگه راز
دست غیب آمد و بر سینهٔ نامحرم زد

دیگران قرعهٔ قسمت همه بر عیش زدند
دل غمدیدهٔ ما بود که هم بر غم زد

جان علوی هوس چاه زنخدان تو داشت
دست در حلقهٔ آن زلف خم اندر خم زد

حافظ آن روز طربنامهٔ عشق تو نوشت
که قلم بر سر اسباب دل خرم زد

All that the Sufi teaches, we must not admire.
His shamful cloak deserves a cleansing fire.

The Sufi with dawn-dregs looked so mellow,
How gay he'll be at night– just watch the fellow.

It is always good to have a touchstone test.
So that hypocrites'sham may manifest.

If from charming Saki's hand wine you drink,
Your faces will become, red, purple and pink.

The wealthy men find no way to the friend,
Only libertines love 's suffering comprehend.

Never mind the mean world; have a drink,
Wise guys should never be worried, I think.

Hafiz, if the Saki another cup 'll make,
Your prayer-rug and cloak, wine-seller 'll take.

INTERPRETATION

*When you listen to speakers, do not follow whatever they say,
for most of the times they are a bit shamful. Use your own discretion.
Try to find out for yourself how truthful these speakers may be.*

*There may be a chance for you to get an exceptional opportunity,
by which you will make outstanding success. But remember that
without strenuous efforts you will not succeed. The difference between
the successful and the unsuccessful is that the former suffers risks and
dangers and wins the battle, whereas the latter leaves the battlefield
halfway through. But keep on trying and cheer up, clearing frowns -
from your forehead. Go ahead steadily and wisely and be careful in
spending your resources for this purpose, for if you run out of funds
then you won't be able to carry on.*

نقد صوفی نه همه صافی بی‌غش باشد   ای بسا خرقه که مستوجب آتش باشد

صوفی ما که ز ورد سحری مست شدی   شامگاهش نگران باش که سرخوش باشد

خوش بود گر محک تجربه آید به میان   تا سیه روی شود هر که در او غش باشد

خط ساقی گر از این گونه زند نقش بر آب   ای بسا رخ که به خونابه منقش باشد

نازپرورد تنعم نبرد راه به دوست   عاشقی شیوهٔ رندان بلاکش باشد

غم دنیی دنی چند خوری باده بخور   حیف باشد دل دانا که مشوش باشد

دل و سجاده حافظ ببرد باده فروش

گر شرابش ز کف ساقی مه‌وش باشد

Seclusion is good, if to Her I've access,
I burn like candle and she enjoys success.

I wouldn't buy a penny, king Solomon's ring,
If occasionally demon's hands may touch the thing.

O Lord! I hope to meet her every day,
But not let her succeed when I'm in dismay.

Where the parrot isn't worth a black kite,
The osprey can't display its grandeur 'n' might.

To show your anxiety, there is no need,
Burning words express, a burning heart indeed.

Your thoughts from my head I can never dispel,
A homesick in his home desires to dwell.

Hafiz, if you had ten tongues like lily,
In her presence as bud you're dumb'n' silly.

INTERPRETATION

If you succeed it is good to keep away from activities for a while. Try not to mix up with bad company, for if you do so, you will depreciate your personal value. Where your personality is not respected, you have no chance to make progress. But you do not need to speak about this to your friends; simply act and by your action show that you excell over them in character and personality.

Although far away, you still cherish the hope of seeing your friend once again. You will do so, but when you see her, you will be so much excited that you will not know how to begin saying something.

خوشت خلوت اگر یا یار من باشد
نه من بسوزم و او شمع انجمن باشد

من آن نگین سلیمان به هیچ نستانم
که گاه گاه بر او دست اهرمن باشد

روا مدار خدایا که در حریم وصال
رقیب محرم و محرم نصیب من باشد

همای گو مفکن سایه شرف هرگز
در آن دیار که طوطی کم از زغن باشد

بیان شوق چه حاجت که سوز آتش دل
توان شناخت ز سوزی که در سخن باشد

هوای کوی تو از سر نمیرود آری
غریب را دل سرگشته با وطن باشد

بسان سوسن اگر ده زبان شود حافظ
چو غنچه پیش تو خاموش مهر بر دهن باشد

107

When the garden displays the fragrant rose,
It's ideal to be cup-in-hand I suppose.

Appreciate your time; enjoy your happy days;
For pearls aren't inside the snail always.

In the rose-garden enjoy time with a drink;
No such clear wine, in paradise, I think.

If you're my schoolmate, all your books conceal,
For science of love none of them will reveal.

Love a real beauty who make- up won't need,
Who is charming without ornaments indeed.

Only those who are to your beauty blind,
To Hafiz's fine poetry objection will find.

INTERPRETATION

Soon you will have a good chance to become successful, and you should make the most of this opportunity. Take full advantage of this opportunity, as such golden opportunity will not be given you often. The success you will gain, will be unique and exceptional. What you will get will not come to you through your education or learning, but through your good sense of judgement and timely decision. What you will get will be well worth a good deal everywhere, without trying to show its real value. You can market it without advertisement etc.

خوش آمد گل وزان خوشتر نباشد   که در دستت بجز ساغر نباشد

زمان خوشدلی دریاب و دریاب   که دایم در صدف گوهر نباشد

غنیمت دان و می خور در گلستان   که گل تا هفته دیگر نباشد

ایا پر دل کرده جام زرین   ببخشا بر کسی کش زر نباشد

بیا ای شیخ و از خمخانه ما   شرابی خور که در کوثر نباشد

بشوی اوراق اگر همدرس مائی   که علم عشق در دفتر نباشد

زمن بنیوش و دل در شاهدی بند   که حسنش بسته زیور نباشد

شرابی بی خمارم بخش یا رب   که با وی هیچ دردی سر نباشد

من از جان بنده سلطان اویسم   اگر چه یادش از چاکر نباشد

بتاج عالم آرایش که خورشید   چنین زیبنده افسر نباشد

کسی گیرد خطا بر نظم حافظ

که هیچش لطف در گوهر نباشد

Once more Zephyr spreads musk by its breeze,
The old world rejuvenated, if you please,

The purple serves jasmine in agate cup;
Narcissus with wonder to anemone looks up.

Separation suffered by nightingale, I suppose ,
Makes it crying until it reaches the rose.

I went from the mosque to tavern in haste,
For Sheikh's sermons I'll have time to waste.

If you put-off today's pleasures to the morrow,
If you don't live, life you cannot borrow.

Flower is dear, enjoy it fully, my moon!
For the garden-flowers will vanish soon.

You've good time, let musicians play,
Forget the future or what passed today.

Hafiz, from birth she was destined for you;
Farewell to her, for soon she'll pass through.

INTERPRETATION

Now there is once more a great chance for you to make success. Everything seems changed, and you have to make the most of the changes for your own benefit. Everything seems to be plentiful and all seem to enjoy them. You must enjoy them too, and forget your disappointments and worries. You will have much time to spend in listening to idle talks— now is the time for your best activities. If you do not make the most of your present opportunities, you may never be able to get such a chance again. Things change quickly and you must take advantage of them when they are available.

Now is the time to enjoy the fruits of your past toils and efforts, and to forget the future. It was your lot to gain this success, so make the most of it, for time flies and things pass quickly.

نفس باد صبا مشک فشان خواهد شد / عالم پیر دگرباره جوان خواهد شد

ارغوان جام عقیقی به سمن خواهد داد / چشم نرگس به شقایق نگران خواهد شد

این تطاول که کشید از غم هجران بلبل / تا سراپرده گل نعره زنان خواهد شد

گر ز مسجد به خرابات شدم خرده مگیر / مجلس وعظ دراز است و زمان خواهد شد

ای دل ار عشرت امروز به فردا فکنی / مایه نقد بقا را که ضمان خواهد شد

ماه شعبان منه از دست قدح کاین خورشید / از نظر تا شب عید رمضان خواهد شد

گل عزیز است غنیمت شمریدش صحبت / که به باغ آمد از این راه و از آن خواهد شد

مطربا مجلس انس است غزل خوان و سرود / چند گویی که چنین رفت و چنان خواهد شد

حافظ از بهر تو آمد سوی اقلیم وجود / قدمی نه به وداعش که روان خواهد شد

Separation day and seclusion night now end;
Take this augury: success on your luck'll depend.

The pride and self-conceit displayed by Fall,
With the approach of Spring, will end all.

By the lucky star of flowers' crown,
Fall winds and annoying thorns were put down.

Twilight of hope twinkles from mystery-curtain;
Dark nights disappeared and victory is certain.

Worries of Winter nights and my heart's grief,
Ended all since her curls brought me relief.

Since time breaches covenant, I can't believe
That good luck of my friend my sorrows 'll relieve.

Saki! On your delightful cup we depend.
Our worries and hangovers your grace'll end.

Though no one for Hafiz consideration had,
Thank God! Transient are both the good and bad.

INTERPRETATION

Good News! Your separation days from the friend will end. Take this as a good augury: Your good luck will bring you success! The great troubles you had in the past will end and a new era of prosperity and happiness will follow. Your success will cause all your opponents to be put down. The twilight of hope twinkles now and soon you will win a great victory. Through the great success you will gain, you will forget all your past strife and efforts which were nerve-racking indeed. But meantime, remember that the slightest mistake on your side, will ruin your luck. So be very careful. If you exercise a little care, all your worries and sorrows will end, and you will enjoy great success.

روز هجران و شب فرقت یار آخر شد   زد مین فال و گذشت اختر و کار آخر شد

آن همه ناز و تنعّم که خزان میفرمود   عاقبت در قدم باد بهار آخر شد

شکر ایزد که به اقبال کلاه گوشهٔ گل   نخوت باد دی و شوکت خار آخر شد

صبح امید که بد معتکف پردهٔ غیب   گو برون آی که کار شب تار آخر شد

آن پریشانی شبهای دراز و غم دل   همه در سایهٔ گیسوی نگار آخر شد

باورم نیست ز بد عهدی ایام هنوز   قصهٔ غصه که در دولت یار آخر شد

ساقیا لطف نمودی قدحت پر می باد   که به تدبیر تو تشویش خمار آخر شد

در شمار ار چه نیاورد کسی حافظ را
شکر کان محنت بی حد و شمار آخر شد

A star appeared becoming our community's moon,
Comforting our disillusioned hearts soon.

My friend went not to school and could not write;
Yet with a blink taught many teachers bright.

The joyous love-home 'll be flourishing again.
Her eyebrow-curve, its cornerstone 'll remain.

Your oglings intoxicated lovers with a wine ,
That its mellowness no wisdom can define.

The verse of Hafiz is as dear as gold,
As elixir welcome by the young and old.

Keep away, my friend from the tavern road,
Hafiz lost everything in that abode.

INTERPRETATION

A great joy is coming to you soon, making your life much brighter than it is now. Though your education is not as high as should be, yet your business background will make good this shortcoming and will enable you to make good success. Once more you will be the center of much attraction, and many people will turn to you. You must avoid spending your time in too much pleasure, for this will ruin your chances and will incur losses on you.

ستاره‌ای بدرخشید و ماه مجلس شد   دل رمیدهٔ ما را رفیق و مونس شد

نگار من که به مکتب نرفت و خط ننوشت   به غمزه مسئله آموز صد مدرس شد

طرب سرای محبت کنون شود معمور   که طاق ابروی یار منش مهندس شد

کرشمهٔ تو شرابی به عاشقان پیمود   که علم بی‌خبر افتاد و عقل بی‌حس شد

چو زر عزیز وجود است نظم من آری   قبول دولتیان کیمیای این مس شد

ز راه میکده یاران عنان بگردانید

چرا که حافظ از این راه رفت و مفلس شد

My soul consumed, but its aim didn't get,
I burned in vain hope; there's no hope yet.

With tears she said: "I will see you tonight"
But she never made my gloomy party bright.

She ordered me a true libertine to be-
Libertine I became but her did not see.

When drunk I hoped her ruby lips to kiss,
Like the cup I drink blood, yet her I miss.

In love's mansion a smart guide you need;
Without a guide we would never succeed.

Alas! Seeking her company 's great pleasure;
Did everything, but didn't get this treasure.

Hafiz, many plans with forethought you made,
Yet her wild heart no attention to you paid.

INTERPRETATION

*You have been working hard to get what you want, but so far
your aim is far away and you think it is a vain hope to expect your wish
done. You expect things to happen every day and night, but it will not
come when you expect it. You try many methods in order to reach
your aim, but to no hope. It has been a very uphill climb for you, the
hope of success being very remote. In this matter you need a very able
and well-informed guide or counsellor, and perhaps this will help you
a bit; but still your chances are one to a hundred.*

گداخت جان که شود کار دل تمام و نشد   بسوختیم در این آرزوی خام و نشد

بلا به گفت شبی میر مجلس تو شوم   شدم به رغبت خویشش کمین غلام و نشد

پیام داد که خواهم نشست با بدان   بشد به رندی و در یکی کشیم نام و نشد

رواست در بر اگر می‌طپد کبوتر دل   که دید در ره خود تاب و پیچ دام و نشد

بدان هوس که به مستی ببوسم آن لب لعل   چه خون که در دلم افتاد همچو جام و نشد

بکوی عشق منه بی دلیل راه قدم   که من بخویش نمودم صد اهتمام و نشد

فغان که در طلب گنج نامه مقصود   شدم خراب جهانی ز غم تمام و نشد

دریغ و درد که در جست و جوی گنج حضور   بسی شدم به گدایی بر کرام و نشد

هزار حیله برانگیخت حافظ از سر فکر
در آن هوس که شود دل به آن نگار رام و نشد

The pious clergy visited the tavern last night;
Ignoring old covenant took wine outright.

Last night the mystic broke the cup insane;
A fresh wine-cup made him sober again.

My beauty dreaming of her youth's days,
Pitying the old man her love displays.

A glow of the rose the nightingale will fry;
Laughing candle burned up the butterfly.

I did not waste morning cry and nightmare-
One of my tears became a pearl so rare.

Saki's narcissus eyes spelled majic,
My incantations are legends tragic.

The home of Hafiz is as a king's court;
The steamer of his heart launched at her port.

INTERPRETATION

You will find that many of your friends forsake you and turn against you. But you will get much closer to your aim, and will find signs of favor and success. Nevertheless, do not forget that because of the achievement in sight, you have to work hard and be prepared for self-sacrifice. If you do that, the chances are that one of your efforts will bring you outstanding results, which will be the result of your efforts and sacrifices. This success will surprise many persons who know about you, as something quite unexpected. The final result will be your total success to such an extent that all the things aspired by you will be yours.

زاهد خلوت نشین دوش بمیخانه شد   از سر پیمان برفت با سر پیمانه شد

صوفی مجلس که دی جام و قدح می‌شکست   باز بیک جرعه می عاقل و فرزانه شد

شاهد عهد شباب آمده بودش بخواب   باز به پیرانه سر عاشق و دیوانه شد

مغبچه‌ای می‌گذشت راهزن دین و دل   در پی آن آشنا از همه بیگانه شد

آتش رخسار گل خرمن بلبل بسوخت   چهرهٔ خندان شمع آفت پروانه شد

گریهٔ شام و سحر شکر که ضایع نگشت   قطرهٔ باران ما گوهر یکدانه شد

نرگس ساقی بخواند آیت افسونگری   حلقهٔ اوراد ما مجلس افسانه شد

منزل حافظ کنون بارگه پادشاست

دل بر دلدار رفت جان بر جانانه شد

119

Good News! My heart, zephyr has come again;
The good-gossip hoopoe, with us 'll remain.

O' Morning bird, sing your beautiful song–
For the king of flowers now comes along.

Where is the Sage, who knows the lily 's tongue–
To ask "Why you went and came? What's wrong?"

I am glad God's grace with me will remain;
For my beautiful moon is loyal again.

Tulip, smelling the scent of wine at dawn,
To heal its sore heart, appeared on the lawn.

My eyes fixed to the road, await the caravan;
When my heart' ll hear, "Lo, she comes on."

Though Hafiz broke his covenant in dismay,
She –full of grace–a visit will soon pay.

INTERPRETATION
Cheer up, for good news come to you again! This good news will continue to come to you for a while. Be happy, for here comes to you a great privilege. You wish you could unfold the secrets and discover why you failed in the past and succeeded now. This time the success you have gained will remain with you for a very long time. But still you expect some greater success. Be sure the next victory will soon come to you.

غزلیات حافظ

مژده ای دل که دگر باد صبا باز آمد   که سلیمان گل از باد هوا باز آمد

برکش ای مرغ سحر نغمهٔ داودی باز   هدهد خوش خبر از طرف سبا باز آمد

عارفی کو که کند فهم زبان سوسن   تا بپرسد که چرا رفت و چرا باز آمد

مردمی کرد و کرم لطف خداداد بمن   کان بت ماه رخ از راه وفا باز آمد

لاله بوی می نوشین بشنید از دم صبح   داغ دل بود به امید دوا باز آمد

چشم من در ره این قافله راه بماند   تا بگوش دلم آواز درا باز آمد

گر چه حافظ در رنجش زد و پیمان بشکست
لطف او بین که بلطف از در ما باز آمد

Zephyr appeared the wine Sage to greet;
So let us all in joyous drinking meet.

The Christ-breath air spread musk on the hill;
The trees are green; the birds sing with a thrill.

The tulip was flourished by wind of Spring;
The bud perspires, the flower is cindering.

Give up dissention and together unite;
When demon disappears the angel comes to sight.

The mysterious voice at dawn cried to say;
"Take my advice–stay happy and gay".

What lily told to the morning bird, I wonder?
With many tongues became quiet to ponder.

For those profane to love there is no place;
Hide the cup when the Sheikh is in disgrace.

Hafiz, your home from mosque to tavern make;
Perhaps from sham's mellowness you will wake.

INTERPRETATION

Pretty soon a message of great importance will come to you. This gives you good reason to be very happy. Everywhere you pass, you will see a new sense of great welcome and readiness to receive you and your proposals. You must work with your collaborators in a spirit of unity and team-work, and this will make your success manyfold. There is every reason for you to be happy, and so keep your spirits high. You can, of course, open your mouth and say many things about other people, but the chances are that they will be annoyed and so it is better for you to keep your mouth closed tight. There are some people who should never be considered as intimate friends, and from whom all secrets should be kept. You will undergo a change soon, which will be to your ultimate benefit, though outwardly it may seem degrading.

صبا به تهنیت پیرمی فروش آمد
که موسم طرب و عیش و ناز و نوش آمد

هوا مسیح نفس گشت و باد نافگشای
درخت سبز شد و مرغ در خروش آمد

تنور لاله چنان برفروخت باد بهار
که غنچه غرق عرق گشت و گل بجوش آمد

بگوش هوش نیوش از من و بشکر بکوش
که این سخن سحر از هاتفم بگوش آمد

ز فکر تفرقه باز آی تا شوی مجموع
بحکم آنکه چو شد اهرمن سروش آمد

ز مرغ صبح ندانم که سوسن آزاد
چه گوش کرد که با ده زبان خموش آمد

چه جای صحبت نامحرمست مجلس انس
سر پیاله بپوشان که خرقه پوش آمد

ز خانقاه بمیخانه میرود حافظ
مگر ز مستی زهد ریا بهوش آمد

At dawn the vigilant luck came to my bed,
"Wake up! The queen of beauties came" It said.

Take a promenade and have a joyous drink;
How glorious she came, one can never think.

Good-news! my intimate scent-spreading friend;
My wild gazelle, some time with me spend.

To my consumed face tears some water brought;
Weeping was good for your lovers, I thought.

My heart is still deep in my beauty's love;
Beware! the Falcon of death comes up, O'Dove!

Saki, serve wine, forget the friend and foe;
Enjoy wine: Foes and friends come and go.

When the infidel Time saw the spring cloud;
Over lily and jonquil wept aloud.

Zephyr heard Hafiz's words from nightingale,
Spread embergris over flowers by gale.

INTERPRETATION

*One early morning you will wake up to hear the good news of the
arrival of a long-expected friend. He or she will come in full glory
and pomp. This friend will remain with you for some time and will
bestow on you great blessings. You must take full advantage of these;
otherwise your chances will be gone soon. Meantime, never fail to be
happy, for friends and foes will come and go. What matters is your
happiness. Besides, a second chance will also be given to you, whereby
great blessings will pour on you.*

124

سحرم دولت بیدار به بالین آمد — گفت برخیز که آن خسرو شیرین آمد

قدحی درکش و سرخوش به تماشا بخرام — تا ببینی که نگارت به چه آیین آمد

مژدگانی بده ای خلوتی نافه گشای — که ز صحرای ختن آهوی مشکین آمد

گریه آبی به رخ سوختگان بازآورد — ناله فریادرس عاشق مسکین آمد

مرغ دل باز هوادار کمان ابروئیست — ای کبوتر نگران باش که شاهین آمد

ساقیا می بده و غم مخور از دشمن و دوست — که به کام دل ما آن بشد و این آمد

رسم بدعهدی ایام چو دید ابر بهار — گریه‌اش بر سمن و سنبل و نسرین آمد

چون صبا گفته حافظ بشنید از بلبل

عنبرافشان به تماشای ریاحین آمد

125

From all beauties capturing hearts don't expect,
All mirrors like Alexander's the world won't reflect.

All who wear costly hats with pride in town;
Are not worthy to get kingdom and crown.

Like the beggars don't worship for reward,
The friend well knows how his servants to regard.

I love libertines who put life at stake;
Who though beggars, elixir of life can make

It's good but hard to be loyal, my lad,
It's much easier to be wicked and bad.

I lost my heart and yet I could not know,
A beauty may manners of fairies show.

Dervishes are not all those who have long hair,
Many secrets exist in this mystic affair.

Of Hafiz's poems only those are aware,
Who for fluent, versatile poetry care.

INTERPRETATION

You will find that all careers are not so well remunerating as yours. Many pretend to be as successful as you, but are not so, and you are an exception. Don't expect to reap results for every action of yours; you may not see the results of some of them. With your empty hand you can do a lot of things that many people with capital and resources cannot do. You are endowed with exceptional talents and resources— use them and be sure they will pay dividends.

126

نه هر که چهره برافروخت دلبری داند

نه هر که آینه سازد سکندری داند

نه هر که طرف کله کج نهاد و تند نشست

کلاه داری و آیین سروری داند

تو بندگی چو گدایان به شرط مزد مکن

که دوست خود روش بنده پروری داند

غلام همت آن رند عافیت سوزم

که در گد اصنعتی کیمیاگری داند

وفا و عهد نکو باشد ار بیاموزی

وگرنه هر که تو بینی ستمگری داند

بباختم دل دیوانه و ندانستم

که آدمی بچه شیوهٔ پری داند

هزار نکته باریکتر ز مو اینجاست

نه هر که سر بتراشد قلندری داند

ز شعر دلکش حافظ کسی بود آگاه

که لطف طبع و سخن گفتن دری داند

Those pure-in-heart, to truth will find their way;
Those ignorant of truth, in denial stay.

Don't object if my secret I cannot hide,
Better exposed than live full of pride.

Sheriff's pious, though in debauchery was bold,
My debaucheries now at street-corners are told.

My heart from eternity to love was true,
Other things perish under the firmament blue.

Narcissus imitated your enchanting eyes,
But failed and so remained in great surprise.

Nothing better than love-tune I cherish,
Such sweet memory the Blue Dome can't perish.

I had a cloak covering all defects of mine;
Alas! It was pawned for music and wine.

Hafiz watched her curl only for one day;
Till eternity in love's bondage 'll stay.

INTERPRETATION

*You must make every effort to have a purer heart and to see
things with a clearer vision. It is much better for you to be exposed
for your weak points than to have pride and sham. You will find that
many people will talk about your activities with criticism, but be sure
you will come out victorious, since you have a pure heart and are
sincere in your intentions. You have been truthful and loyal and this
will wipe off the effects of any criticism. Be sure the world will turn
to your favor, since you know you are honest in your ways. So you
will continue to be respected and appreciated throughout your life.*

هرکه شد محرم دل در حرم یار بماند   وآنکه این کار ندانست در انکار بماند

اگر از پرده برون شد دل من عیب مکن   شکر ایزد که نه در پرده پندار بماند

محتسب شیخ شد و فسق خود از یاد ببرد   قصه ماست که در هر سر بازار بماند

بر دل من گر از ازل تا به ابد عاشق رفت   جاودان کس نشنیدیم که در کار بماند

گشت بیمار که چون چشم تو گردد نرگس   شیوه تو نشدش حاصل و بیمار بماند

از صدای سخن عشق ندیدم خوشتر   یادگاری که در این گنبد دوار بماند

داشتم دلقی و صد عیب مرا می‌پوشید   خرقه رهن می و مطرب شد و زنار بماند

به تماشاگه زلفش دل حافظ روزی

شد که بازآید و جاوید گرفتار بماند

Good news! Ended days of sorrow and pain;
It was never so, and will never so remain.

Though before the friend I was worthless as the dust;
My rival also will soon be down-thrust.

Bad luck doesn't cause me any mental strain,
In the book of existence no records will remain.

At King Jam's party this song was cherished,
"Enjoy your wine, for Jam will be perished!"

O' candle enjoy the love of your butterfly,
For, till morning only this you can try.

Enrich your heart, O' wealthy man! Behold,
Your treasures of gold you can never hold.

Hafiz, for your friend's love, never mind,
The time will come when love you won't find.

INTERPRETATION

Good news for you! Your days of sorrow and pain will soon end. But as you know, things may change again, as the world is always changing. If you had a hard time to win your battle, your competitors had a much harder time. The world being so transient, you should not fail to spend your time with the best available company. Enjoy your present successes to the fullest extent, for no one knows how long it may last. Besides acquiring wealth, try also to acquire knowledge and self-sufficiency, for treasures of gold may perish, but the treasure of self-sufficiency always lasts. So always be happy.

رسیده مژده که ایام غم نخواهد ماند   چنان نماند چنین نیز هم نخواهد ماند

من ار چه در نظر یار خاکسار شدم   رقیب نیز چنین محترم نخواهد ماند

چو پرده دار به شمشیر می‌زند همه را   کسی مقیم حریم حرم نخواهد ماند

چه جای شکر و شکایت ز نقش نیک و بد است   چو بر صحیفهٔ هستی رقم نخواهد ماند

سرود مجلس جمشید گفته‌اند این بود   که جام باده بیاور که جم نخواهد ماند

غنیمتی شمر ای شمع وصل پروانه   که این معامله تا صبحدم نخواهد ماند

توانگرا دل درویش خود به دست آور   که مخزن زر و گنج درم نخواهد ماند

بدین رواق زبرجد نوشته‌اند به زر   که جز نکویی اهل کرم نخواهد ماند

ز مهربانی جانان طمع مبر حافظ   که نقش جور و نشان ستم نخواهد ماند

Last night at dawn I was relieved from grief;
I was granted the water-of-life in brief.

In ecstacy God's manifestation I could see;
The transformation cup was given to me.

What a blessed and what a glorious night!
A unique experience and a wonderful sight!

In mirror of God's beauty my face did shine;
To me were unfolded many secrets divine.

No wonder that in spirit I feel sublime;
For I needed blessings–they came in time.

"Good news! Great fortune" mysterious voice says;
That's why I can suffer all her cunning ways.

All the honey that drips from my tongue,
Was my beauty's reward for suffering so long.

Hafiz's ambition and pious prayers of the morn;
Relieved me from sorrow, enmity and scorn.

INTERPRETATION

You have now received a great blessing, which will change the whole course of life. A great change is taking place in you and your life. It will change everything in your life. God is manifesting to you and you will experience many divine blessings. You feel very much exalted and rightly so, for God's blessings came to you just when you needed them most. Great fortune and great happiness will come to you and these blessings will enable you to withstand the greatest temptations. These blessings were bestowed on you because you waited so long and worked so hard and patiently. Your earnest prayers and efforts saved you from all sorrow, enmity and scorn.

دوش وقت سحر از غصه نجاتم دادند   و اندر آن ظلمت شب آب حیاتم دادند

بخود از پرتو ذاتم کردند   باده از جام تجلی صفاتم دادند

چه مبارک سحری بود و چه فرخنده شبی   آن شب قدر که این تازه براتم دادند

بعد از این روی من و آینه وصف جمال   که در آنجا خبر از جلوه ذاتم دادند

من اگر کامروا گشتم و خوشدل چه عجب   مستحق بودم و اینها بزکاتم دادند

هاتف آن روز به من مژده این دولت داد   که بدان جور و جفا صبر و ثباتم دادند

این همه شهد و شکر کز سخنم میریزد   اجر صبریست کزان شاخ نباتم دادند

همت حافظ و انفاس سحرخیزان بود

که ز بند غم ایام نجاتم دادند

The angels knocked at the tavern-door last night,
With man's clay, they kneaded the cup outright.

The dwellers of God's heavenly abode,
Drank wine with me—a beggar of the road.

Heaven could not bear this wonderful trust,
That to a madman this honor was thrust.

Disputes of religions is but a false pretense,
Having not seen the Truth, they speak nonsense.

Thank God! There is peace between Him and me.
So dancing mystics took their cups with glee.

What makes the candle laughing isn't a flame.
The fire that burned the butterfly is my aim.

No one can display thoughts as Hafiz can,
No such words are written by the pen of man.

INTERPRETATION

You will soon be lifted up to a very high position, spending your time with the top-level people of your society. This honor bestowed on you will be exceptional. If one believes in God and is truthful in his religion, he must respect all other religions, remembering that all of them worship the same God and try to purify the hearts of mankind in different ways.

Cheer up, for you will enjoy a period of peace and tranquility, and many people will be happy for that. Meantime remember that the reason you were conferred this honor was that you had a great zeal and enthusiasm and worked with all sincerity and perseverance. So keep up this good habit.

دوش دیدم که ملایک در میخانه زدند   گل آدم بسرشتند و به پیمانه زدند

ساکنان حرم ستر و عفاف ملکوت   با من راه نشین باده مستانه زدند

آسمان بار امانت نتوانست کشید   قرعه کار بنام من دیوانه زدند

جنگ هفتاد و دو ملت همه را عذر بنه   چون ندیدند حقیقت ره افسانه زدند

شکر ایزد که میان من و او صلح افتاد   صوفیان رقص کنان ساغر شکرانه زدند

آتش آن نیست که از شعله او خندد شمع   آتش آنست که در خرمن پروانه زدند

کس چو حافظ نگشاد از رخ اندیشه نقاب

تا سر زلف سخن را به قلم شانه زدند

135

O' Heart! Your suffering, miracles will do.
Midnight prayers solve all problems for you.

Suffer your friend's tyrannies, for to a lover-true,
The friend's ogling all her tyrannies will do.

Before servitors of the true wine of love,
There are no veils on earth or Heaven above.

The love-physician as Christ all troubles heals,
But where there is no pain no remedy appeals.

My sleepy heart! Wake and tell those awake,
Prayers for me at twilight time to make.

Hafiz consumed; of friend's curl, there's no trace,
Zephyr will lead me to his mansion o' grace.

INTERPRETATION

Be sure your hard efforts and sufferings will bring you miraculous esults. Keep on praying earnestly, for all your problems will be solved. 'f you suffer the hardships with a patient attitude, the success you gain will be so great that will recompense all your past efforts. There is no obstacle that cannot be surpassed by a man of decision and ambition.

دلا بسوز که سوز تو کارها بکند   نیاز نیم شبی دفع صد بلا بکند

عتاب یار پری چهره عاشقانه بکش   که یک کرشمه تلافی صد جفا بکند

ز ملک تا ملکوتش حجاب بردارند   هر آنکه خدمت جام جهان نما بکند

طبیب عشق مسیحا دم است و مشفق لیک   چو درد در تو نبیند کرا دوا بکند

تو با خدای خود انداز کار و دل خوش دار   که رحم اگر نکند مدعی خدا بکند

ز بخت خفته ملولم بود که بیداری   بوقت فاتحه صبح یک دعا بکند

بسوخت حافظ و بوئی بزلف یار نبرد

مگر دلالت این دولتش صبا بکند

The ignorant is perplexed that my love I show;
I am what I'm—let the whole world know.

Only for lovers this globe turns in speed;
All those without love are vagrants indeed.

His beauty is not witnessed by my eyes alone;
It is reflected in the Moon and the Sun.

God at eternity my covenant with beauties sealed,
All my sufferings by beauties will be healed.

Though I'm poor; myself rich with wine I make;
But my woolly cloak for pawn they won't take.

The blind butterfly to the Sun can never get;
No wisdom has understood God's mystery yet.

No true lover can God complain,
Such lovers always distant will remain.

If Zephyr leads you to the spiritual kingdom,
It is worth to give your soul as ransom.

Hypocrites the libertine Hafiz don't understand,
The word of God demons cannot expand.

INTERPRETATION

*Many people may wonder how outrageous in your sentiments
and ways you are. Let them wonder, for you cannot change your ways.
Besides, only such courageous attitudes may bring forth good results.
Those who lack it, are wasting their time.*

*Meantime, please remember that your ambitions should also have
limits, and you cannot fly too high. It is really worth to make every
sacrifice for the aim you have in mind, for it is worth any and all your
efforts. Let people wonder at your outstanding bravery and spirit of
adventure —they do not understand you— are on the right track, to
success.*

در نظر بازی ما بی‌خبران حیرانند
من چنینم که نمودم دگر ایشان دانند

عاقلان نقطهٔ پرگار وجودند ولی
عشق داند که در این دایره سرگردانند

جلوه‌گاه رخ او دیدهٔ من تنهانیست
ماه و خورشید همین آینه می‌گردانند

عهد ما با لب شیرین دهنان بست خدا
ما همه بنده و این قوم خداوندانند

مفلسانیم و هوای می و مطرب داریم
آه اگر خرقهٔ پشمین بگرو نستانند

وصل خورشید بشب پرهٔ اعمی نرسد
که در آن آینه صاحب نظران حیرانند

لاف عشق و گله از یار زهی لاف دروغ
عشقبازان چنین سستی عهده مجرمانند

گر بمستگه ارواح برو بوی تو باد
عقل و جان گو بهر هستی بنثارافشانند

زاهد ار رندی حافظ نکند فهم چه شد
دیو بگریزد از آن قوم که قرآن خوانند

139

Enchanted by your eyes is even the King;
Your lips to sober men intoxication bring.

Zephyr secrets of your beauty 'll display,
Just as my tears my love will soon betray.

When you pass by with your two-fold hair,
Pity your lovers weeping all in despair.

Zephyr caressed violets; come and witness;
Your curls' ravage caused people distress.

O' Sheikh! Why don't I deserve paradise?
The sinner and pious deserve mercy likewise.

Auspicious nightingale! Near me abide;
I walk alone, while her followers ride.

Come to tavern and purple face with wine;
Forget ascetics—their deeds are not divine.

Under your curly locks let Hafiz remain,
Those under your snare, salvation gain.

INTERPRETATION

You have many causes of attraction, which means that many people of respect and dignity will focus their attention to you. Meantime look out, for your secrets may be divulged against your will. There will be many who need your help and favor, and you should not turn your face away from them, rather try to please and convince them that you have a kind heart for all. For a while you will feel a sense of loneliness, as other people will attract the attention of most of your friends. Never mind and cheer up, for with your means you are certain to succeed and to gain great salvation out of your troubles.

غلام نرگس مست تو تاجدارانند		خراب باده لعل تو هوشیارانند
ترصبا ومراآب دیده شد غماز		وگرنه عاشق ومعشوق رازدارانند
زیر زلف دوتا چون گذر کنی بنگر		که از یمین ویسارت چه سوگوارانند
گذار کن چو صبا بر بنفشه زار و ببین		که از تطاول لعفت چه بیقرارانند
نصیب ماست بهشت ای خداشناس برو		که مستحق کرامت گناهکارانند
نه من بر آن گل عارض غزل سرایم وبس		که عندلیب توازهر طرف هزارانند
تو دستگیر شوای خضر پی خجسته که من		پیاده میروم وهمرهان سوارانند
بیا بیسکند و چهره ارغوانی کن		مرو بصومعه کانجا سیاه کارانند
خلاص حافظ از آن زلف تابدار مبا
که بستگان کمند تو رستگارانند

Those who by a glance turn the dust to gold;
Should care for Hafiz though forsaken and old.

Better hide from rival physicians my pain;
Perhaps from divine treasure cure I gain.

When my friend does not uncover his face,
People should not try him in vain to trace.

Whether good or bad, our ends are the same,
Let's ask the Lord our destinies to frame.

Don't be ignorant, since in love's kingdom,
Those who are learned respect men of wisdom,

Behind the curtain seditions go on;
But the destiny of man is known to none.

It is really better to be a sinner great,
Than worship God in a shamful state.

Come to tavern for pure-hearted drinkers may,
For your success and happiness pray.

Hafiz! Of her steadfast love despair,
For king's favor to the poor is so rare.

INTERPRETATION

Though you are of some age, and do not expect great things to happen, yet there will come to you a great blessing. Don't let your competitors know of your weak points, for there is a chance that God will help you. Work hard and trust the Lord and you will get what you are after. You must increase your knowledge and learning about your specific line.

In your career try to be sincere and without sham, for your simple manners will attract people more than the hypocrites.

Meantime, remember that if success comes to you, it will be a rare occasion and will not be often repeated.

آنان که خاک را بنظر کیمیا کنند / آیا بود که گوشهٔ چشمی بما کنند

دردم نهفته به ز طبیبان مدعی / باشد که از خزانهٔ غیبم دوا کنند

معشوق چون نقاب ز رخ در نمی‌کشد / هر کس حکایتی بتصور چرا کنند

چون حسن عاقبت نه برندی و زاهدیست / آن به که کار خود به عنایت رها کنند

بی معرفت مباش که در من یزید عشق / اهل نظر معامله با آشنا کنند

حالی درون پرده بسی فتنه میرود / تا آن زمان که پرده برافتد چها کنند

گر سنگ ازین حدیث بنالد عجب مدار / صاحب‌دلان حکایت دل خوش ادا کنند

می خور که صد گناه ز اغیار در حجاب / بهتر ز طاعتی که به روی و ریا کنند

پیراهنی که آید از او بوی یوسفم / ترسم برادران غیورش قبا کنند

بگذر بکوی میکده تا زمرهٔ حضور / اوقات خود ز بهر تو صرف دعا کنند

پنهان ز حاسدان بخودم خوان که منعمان / خیر نهان برای رضای خدا کنند

حافظ دوام وصل میسر نمیشود / شاهان کم التفات بحال گدا کنند

I asked "When my lips will meet my desire?"
She said "Soon! they will do what you aspire".

"A heavy price" I said, "your lips will ask".
She said" still a beneficial task."

"To your lips" I said, "who can find his way?"
"Only wisemen," she said" this game 'll play."

I said: "Worship no idols— in God abide"
"Never mind" she said , "Love is your guide."

"Your pains" I said "the tavern takes away".
"Blessed are those" said she, "who remain gay"

I said, "Wine and cloak religion reprimands"
She replied" Let's do as the Sage commands."

I asked, "What old men from ruby lips take?"
"Kisses" she said, "old men young 'll make."

I asked, "Shall I really meet you soon?"
She said, "Yes, when conjoin Jupiter and Moon."

I said "Hafiz prays for success of you"
"This" she replied, "angels of Heaven do".

INTERPRETATION

Soon you will get what you aspire. This will cost you dear, but it is worth the price. Stay happy and complete your successes with much happiness. The success you gain, will change the whole aspect of your life, and you will look much younger because of it. Nevertheless, you expect certain things that are most difficult to get , almost like an impossibility. But still keep on working for it.

گفتم دهان و لبت کامران کنند ← گفتا بچشم هر چه تو گوئی چنان کنند

گفتم خراج مصر طلب میکند لبت ← گفت این معامله کمتر زیان کنند

گفتم بنقطهٔ دهنت که برد راه ← گفت این حکایتیست که با نکته دان کنند

گفتم صنم پرست مشو با صمد نشین ← گفتا بکوی عشق همین و همان کنند

گفتم هوای میکده غم میبرد ز دل ← گفتا خوش آن کسان که دلی شادمان کنند

گفتم شراب و خرقه نه آیین مذهب است ← گفت این عمل بمذهب پیر مغان کنند

گفتم ز لعل نوش لبان پیر را چه سود ← گفتا ببوسهٔ شکرینش جوان کنند

گفتم که خواجه کی بسر حجله میرود ← گفت آنزمان که مشتری و مه قران کنند

گفتم دعای دولت او ورد حافظ است ← گفت این دعا ملایک هفت آسمان کنند

145

On pulpit or in altar, preachers preach,
But secretly act contrary to what they teach.

I have a question of my pious man;
"Why preach repentance, when repent never can?"

Preachers do not believe in judgement day,
Since the Judge's orders they never obey.

O' Covenant mendicant! At tavern they give,
Heart-flourishing water— come and receive.

His tempting beauty if lovers can stand;
Revelations of love they may understand.

Angels! Worship the love-temple divine—
For Adam's clay is kneaded there with wine.

"A Clamour 's heard in Heaven", said wisdom;
"Hafiz's verse 's sung by saints of kingdom."

INTERPRETATION

You should not ask people to abstain from what you cannot yourself abstain. Indeed, most people make this great mistake. You have a good chance to get some brilliant success, which will be envied by many. Stick to it and you will get it. There will come a time when your name and your deeds will be spoken of by all the people. All will praise you and your success.

واعظان کاین جلوه در محراب و منبر میکنند

چون بخلوت میروند آن کار دیگر میکنند

مشکلی دارم ز دانشمند مجلس بازپرس

توبه فرمایان چرا خود توبه کمتر میکنند

گوییا باور نمیدارند روز داوری

کاین همه قلب و دغل در کار داور میکنند

یارب این نودولتان را با خر خودشان نشان

کاین همه ناز از غلام ترک و استر میکنند

ای گدای خانقه برجه که در دیر مغان

میدهند آبی که دلها را توانگر میکنند

حسن بی پایان او چندانکه عاشق میکشد

زمره دیگر بعشق از غیب سر بر میکنند

بر در میخانه عشق ای ملک تسبیح گوی

کاندر آنجا طینت آدم مخمر میکنند

صبحدم از عرش می آمد خروشی عقل گفت

قدسیان گویی که شعر حافظ از بر میکنند

This is what the lyre cries to say I think,
"If openly criticised, secretly drink."

"The Sheikhs condemn love and all lovers bold,
"They condemn all — both young and old. "

"They ban love-secret to hear and to tell-"
"My choice is love, even if I go to Hell."

They have nothing but dark hearts and still,
Proudly believe miracles they fulfill.

Outside the curtain we're fooled in many ways,
No one knows what God the almighty says.

They blindly order men to avoid the Sage,
They show no respect for men of old age.

Many kingdoms of hearts are bought by a glance,
Beauties are guilty for ignoring this chance.

Some try by ascetism to reach God's gate,
Others for success depend on their fate.

On the transient world you can't depend,
All its past deeds the world 'll change 'n' amend.

Hafiz, drink; Sheikh and Sheriff, I tell,
Are all hypocrites, if you examine them well.

INTERPRETATION

You may find that you are criticised by some persons of social standing. Never mind, this, BUT KEEP ON TO DO GOOD AND TO BE GOOD. If you want to live according to what other people recommend, then your life would be entirely different from what it is now. Stick to your own ways and be sure your benevolent heart will reap results. Your good behavior and kindly attitude may bring you numerous benefits. Don't give up this attitude. Since the world is changing all the time, you should, therefore, realise that your situation too— good or bad— will change.

دانی که چنگ و عود چه تقریر میکنند   پنهان خورید باده که تعزیر میکنند

ناموس عشق و رونق عشاق میبرند   عیب جوان و سرزنش پیر میکنند

جز قلب تیره هیچ نشد حاصل و هنوز   باطل درین خیال که اکسیر میکنند

گویند رمز عشق مگویید و مشنوید   مشکل حکایتیست که تقریر میکنند

ما از برون در شده مغرور صد فریب   تا خود درون پرده چه تدبیر میکنند

تشویش وقت پیر مغان میدهند باز   این سالکان نگر که چه با پیر میکنند

صد ملک دل به نیم نظر میتوان خرید   خوبان درین معامله تقصیر میکنند

قومی بجد و جهد نهادند وصل دوست   قومی دگر حواله به تقدیر میکنند

فی الجمله اعتماد مکن بر ثبات دهر   کاین کارخانه ایست که تغییر میکنند

می خور که شیخ و حافظ و مفتی و محتسب
چون نیک بنگری همه تزویر میکنند

I hope wide opens again the tavern door,
And sham's tricks are exposed once more.

If the tavern is closed by clergy's whim,
It will be again opened in the name of Him.

My heart—though a libertine— is so pure,
My prayers open closed doors, I am sure.

Give condolence to the virgin of vine,
For dischevelled their ringlets, all sellers of wine.

At the wine death-bed the harp pulled its hair,
Lest of its deep worries opponents be aware.

O'Lord! The tavern's closed but don't permit,
That wide open remain, gate of the hypocrite.

Hafiz! Many wear your cloak, but tomorrow may,
To the cross or idol shamfully pray.

INTERPRETATION

You expect to have another chance to succeed; you will have it and this time with greater respect. Your pure heart and good efforts will open many closed doors before you. You may face a defeat, but your opponents will also suffer a defeat. Your good intentions and benevolence will help you out.

بود آیا که در میکده‌ها بگشایند   گره از کار فروبستهٔ ما بگشایند

اگر از بهر دل زاهد خودبین بستند   دل قوی دار که از بهر خدا بگشایند

به صفای دل رندان صبوحی زدگان   بس در بسته به مفتاح دعا بگشایند

نامهٔ تعزیت دختر رز بنویسید   تا همه مغبچگان زلف دوتا بگشایند

گیسوی چنگ ببرید به مرگ می ناب   تا حریفان همه خون از مژه‌ها بگشایند

در میخانه ببستند خدایا مپسند   که در خانهٔ تزویر و ریا بگشایند

حافظ این خرقه که داری تو ببینی فردا

که چه زنار ز زیرش به دغا بگشایند

So long as of wine and tavern is trace,
My head will be ransomed at the Sage's pace.

As "Sage-devotee" fore'er 's recorded my name,
I am faithful and continue to be the same.

If you pass by my grave, remember to pray,
For carousels' pilgrimage will be my clay.

My beauty who killed lovers was drunk today;
Who is going to be her love's next prey!?.

O' selfish Sheikh, neither your eyes nor mine.,
Will ever unfold secrets of the divine.

My eyes with your love lie in grave with pain,
Till eternity gazing they will remain.

Hafiz! If you so unhappy remain,
Possession of her curls others may gain.

INTERPRETATION

One of your good attributes is faithfulness or loyalty. Keep up to this high standard. It will cause many people to respect and remember you with great reverence. This loyalty may cost you very dear, and may deprive you of many privileges, but the self-satisfaction you get from it is worth more than all the expected privileges. You may not succeed to get what you want, but you will be proud of your own high standards during all your life and will never regret to have lost so much for sticking to your high principles.

تا زین خانه و می نام و نشان خواهد بود — سر ما خاک ره پیر مغان خواهد بود

حلقهٔ پیر مغان از ازلم در گوش است — بر همانیم که بودیم و همان خواهد بود

بر سر تربت ما چون گذری همت خواه — که زیارتگه رندان جهان خواهد بود

برو ای زاهد خودبین که ز چشم من و تو — راز این پرده نهانست و نهان خواهد بود

ترک عاشق کش من مست برون رفت امروز — تا دگر خون که از دیده روان خواهد بود

چشمم آن دم که ز شوق تو نهد سر به لحد — تا دم صبح قیامت نگران خواهد بود

بخت حافظ گر از این گونه مدد خواهد کرد — زلف معشوقه به دست دگران خواهد بود

To those who seek you hard, without despair,
If you're unkind, it is really unfair.

Your tyranny O'friend! never expect,
You don't do what in true faith 's incorrect.

Eyes without love-tears better be blind,
A heart without some love, gloomy you will find.

The bird of happiness fortune 'll bring,
Ravens and kites never give you such a thing.

Don't criticise, if to the Sage I appeal,
The clergy preached, "In mosque there's no zeal".

Without truth pagoda and church are the same;
A house without piety has no good name.

Hafiz! With wisdom and learning remain!
Or else divine company you never gain.

INTERPRETATION

Some people are working very hard for you and with great enthusiasm, and you should show more consideration and favor towards them. Trusting that you always want to do things right, it is certain that you will correct your mistakes in this respect. Remember that high standards will bring you fortune. So, hitch your wagon to the stars and have high aims. It is not the place of worship that counts much, but the spirit of worship that matters. If you seek divine guidance improve your wisdom and spiritual insight.

خستگان را چو طلب باشد و قوت نبود / گر تو بیدادکنی شرط مروت نبود

ما جفا از تو ندیدیم و تو خود نپسندی / آنچه در مذهب ارباب طریقت نبود

خیره آن دیده که آبش نبرد گریهٔ عشق / تیره آن دل که در او شمع محبت نبود

دولت از مرغ همایون طلب و سایهٔ او / زانکه با زاغ و زغن شهپر دولت نبود

گر مدد خواستم از پیر مغان عیب مکن / شیخ ما گفت که در صومعه همت نبود

چون طهارت نبود کعبه و بتخانه یکیست / نبود خیر در آن خانه که عصمت نبود

حافظا علم و ادب ورز که در مجلس شاه / هر که را نیست ادب لایق صحبت نبود

Last night the story of your locks was told,
Till dawn secrets of your curls did unfold.

My heart, though bleeding by your lash's dart,
Was unwilling from your brows-curve to depart.

God bless Zephyr! message from her it brought,
For how to get her news, I never thought.

People have not realised her love's thrill,
Though her oglings attempted many to kill.

Once I was so secure; now I'm astray.
Her black curls were traps laid on my life's way.

Cast your garment off and revive my soul,
For in the game of life you are my goal .

Be loyal and pass by Hafiz's clay,
For with your thoughts Hafiz has passed away.

INTERPRETATION

Though you may be a little unfair to certain friends, yet they will be much devoted and attached to you. When you are hopeless of your own case, you will hear unexpected good news. You may think that once you ran no risks and were so secure, but bear in mind that those risks have made you as successful as you are and will help you still more in future. So, keep on doing what you did in the past and be sure you will succeed.

دوش در حلقهٔ ما قصهٔ گیسوی تو بود
تا دل شب سخن از سلسلهٔ موی تو بود

دل که از ناوک مژگان تو در خون می‌گشت
باز مشتاق کمانخانهٔ ابروی تو بود

هم عفاالله صبا کز تو پیامی می‌داد
ورنه در کس نرسیدیم که از کوی تو بود

عالم از شور و شر عشق خبر هیچ نداشت
فتنه انگیز جهان غمزهٔ جادوی تو بود

من سرگشته هم از اهل سلامت بودم
دام راهم شکن طرهٔ هندوی تو بود

بگشا بند قبا تا بگشاید دل من
که گشادی که مرا بود ز پهلوی تو بود

به وفای تو که بر تربت حافظ بگذر
کز جهان می‌شد و در آرزوی روی تو بود

157

Sweet dream I had :- Wine -cup I retain,
Its interpretation is :- Success I gain!.

Forty years I worked hard with much strife,
On two-year-old wine now depends my life.

I asked fortune, musk of success to give,
It said "This, in folds of her curls receive."

The hangover of grief took me at twilight,
But fortune filled my cup with wine so bright.

At the tavern always my blood I drink;
This was my lot, at destiny-desk I think.

If the seeds of benevolence you don't sow,
As lilies distorted by Zephyr you will go.

At dawn when to the rose-garden I went,
The morning-bird with love-cries its life spent.

In His praise the verse of Hafiz began,
A stanza of it better than books, my man.

INTERPRETATION

You will gain success, as you can see from this verse. Having worked hard for some time, now you are reaping the sweet first fruits of your toils and troubles. You had searched many years what you get and enjoy now.   After many troublesome and stormy years, you will get what you have aspired, which is a great blessing.

In all your efforts try to be benevolent and well-intending towards your fellow human beings; otherwise, your evil thoughts will re-act on your own life.

دیدم بخواب خوش که بدستم پیاله بود
تعبیر رفت و کار بدولت حواله بود

چل سال رنج و غصه کشیدیم و عاقبت
تدبیر ما بدست شراب دوساله بود

آن نافه مراد که می خواستم ز بخت
در چین زلف آن بت مشکین کلاله بود

از دست برده بود مرا خمار غم سحر
دولت مساعد آمد و می در پیاله بود

بر آستان میکده خون می خورم مدام
روزی ما ز خوان قدر این نواله بود

هر کو نکاشت مهر و ز خوبی گلی نچید
در رهگذار باد نگهبان لاله بود

بر طرف گلشنم گذر افتاد وقت صبح
آندم که کار مرغ سحر آه و ناله بود

دیدیم شعر دلکش حافظ بمدح شاه
یک بیت ازین قصیده به از صد رساله بود

آن شاه تند حمله که خورشید شیر گیر
پیشش برو ز معرکه کمتر غزاله بود

159

Brethren! Once a very intimate heart I had,
Confided it secrets–both good and bad .

When in trouble, melancholy and sore,
My heart led me then to the safety shore.

A sympathetic heart and a friend so wise,
All men of truth it endeavoured to advise.

But I lost it in the home of the friend,
What an overwhelming love, I can't comprehend!

All men are expected unhappy to be,
No one in this world is as unhappy as me.

O' friend, pity this withered spirit of mine,
For once it was exalted and so fine.

Only when love taught me words to express,
My love-story was told all, I confess.

Let us say no more "Hafiz wisdom had,"
For you see he is ignorant and mad.

INTERPRETATION

You have lost a good deal in the course of your career, sometimes even you seem to have lost all your wits. You may think you are the unhappiest person in the world because of these hardships. You are still expecting some miraculous events to happen, perhaps something will happen that will change the course of events in your life. Work hard and that miracle may take place.

مسلمانان مرا وقتی دلی بود   که با وی گفتمی گر مشکلی بود

مگر دایی چو می افتادم از غم   بتد بریرش امید ساحلی بود

دلی همدرد و یاری مصلحت بین   که استظهار هر اهل دلی بود

ز من ضایع شد اندر کوی جانان   چه دامن گیر یا رب منزلی بود

هنر بی عیب حرمان نیست لیکن   ز من محروم ترکی سائلی بود

برین جان پریشان رحمت آرید   که وقتی کاردانی کاملی بود

مرا تا عشق تعلیم سخن کرد   حدیثم نکته هر محفلی بود

مگو دیگر که حافظ نکته دانست

که ما دیدیم و محکم جاهلی بود

My tears will betray my sorrow I fear;
My hidden love to all the world 'll appear.

"Patience turns stones to rubies", they say.
Yes! If you work hard and wait long, it may.

With tears I ask the tavern justice to give,
Perhaps at the tavern, sorrows 'll relieve.

Prayer-darts to all directions I send;
Perhaps one hits the target I intend.

Whisper my love-story to the friend,
Secretly — lest Zephyr may comprehend.

Elixir of God's love turned to gold my face;
Yea! Dust will transmute to gold by grace.

So indignant of rivals' pride I became,
O'Lord, don't let mean persons enjoy fame.

Many things besides beauty are required;
To capture those who are love-inspired.

Turmoil brewing at the turret of the friend,
Will turn many heads to dust in the end.

Hafiz! Hold fast her musked curls in hand.
Hush! For if Zephyr hears, it may demand.

INTERPRETATION

You feel that you have worked hard for many years and, have not reaped the fruits you expect to get. But remember that the success you expect is really substantial, and that only by patience and hard work you can get it. But be sure you will get it, though it may take a while. You are now doing everything humanly possible, not neglecting to crown your deeds with earnest prayers. Be sure one of these will work out. God's grace will turn all your efforts to fruitful results. Remember, to gain success, you should possess exceptional qualities.

ترسم که اشک در غم ما پرده در شود   وین راز سر به مهر به عالم سمر شود

گویند سنگ لعل شود در مقام صبر   آری شود ولیک به خون جگر شود

خواهم شدن به میکده گریان و دادخواه   کز دست غم خلاص من آنجا مگر شود

از هر کرانه تیر دعا کرده‌ام روان   باشد کز آن میانه یکی کارگر شود

ای جان حدیث ما بر دلدار باز گو   لیکن چنان مگو که صبا را خبر شود

از کیمیای مهر تو زر گشت روی من   آری به یمن لطف شما خاک زر شود

در تنگنای حیرتم از نخوت رقیب   یا رب مباد آن که گدا معتبر شود

بس نکته غیر حسن بباید که تا کسی   مقبول طبع مردم صاحب نظر شود

این سرکشی که کنگره کاخ وصل راست   سرها بر آستانه او خاک در شود

حافظ چو نافه سر زلفش به دست توست   دم درکش ار نه با صبا را خبر شود

Though to the preacher this advice is hard;
If you're a hypocrite, your faith brings no reward.

Libertines may be pious; it isn't strange;
Brutes by true love to humans 'll change.

Only genuine jewel 's worthy of praise,
Stones and clays in value never raise.

O Heart! God's love will pour blessings on thee,
Demons by cunning skill faithful can't be.

I seek love,hoping that this divine source,
Like other sources won't bring me remorse.

I ask God to give her a good humor,
That she may not break my heart any more.

Hafiz, as a molecule having high aim,
Prestige of the Sun you desire to claim.

INTERPRETATION

It may not be liked by you, but you should always fight against hypocrisy in yourself and others. True love may transform the crudest persons into angels.

Don't seek things that are low in value, in your efforts; rather try to attain some thing worthy of achieving. Be sure, God will pour his blessings on you; and your campaign will result in great benefits for you. Of course, you expect that this will be your final success and that you will not have any more failures, but this may not be so. You are striving hard to climb up to the heights of supremacy, and this ambition in itself is worthy of praise, plus the fact that you have a great chance of progress.

گرچه بر واعظ شهر این سخن آسان نشود   تا ریا ورزد و سالوس مسلمان نشود

رندی آموز و کرم کن که نه چندان هنر است   حیوانی که ننوشد می و انسان نشود

گوهر پاک بباید که شود قابل فیض   ورنه هر سنگ و گلی لؤلؤ و مرجان نشود

اسم اعظم بکند کار خود ای دل خوش باش   که به تلبیس و حیل دیو سلیمان نشود

عشق می ورزم و امید که این فن شریف   چون هنرهای دگر موجب حرمان نشود

دوش می گفت که فردا بدهم کام دلت   سببی ساز خدایا که پشیمان نشود

حسن خلقی ز خدا می طلبم خوی ترا   تا دگر خاطر ما از تو پریشان نشود

ذره را تا نبود همت عالی حافظ

طالب چشمه خورشید درخشان نشود

I said "I'm love-sick", she said "will end".
"My moon"? said I. She said "Do not depend."

"From lovers" I said, "learn loyalty and care."
"Such things" she replied "in beauties are rare."

"I will close my eyes, to avoid you, " I say.
"Nocturnal thief" she said. "comes another way."

"Scent of your locks, "I said, "leads me astray."
"Be wise" she said, "it only shows the way."

I said "Fresh air the morning breeze 'll send".
She said "It's from the home of the friend."

I said " Will your ruby lips me relieve?
She said, "Servitors I only receive."

"Your tender heart" said I, "reconcile will?"
She said "Keep on waiting and keep still."

I said, "Sweet days pass quickly, you see."
She said, "Hafiz, worries, too, soon cease to be."

INTERPRETATION

Your period of patience and waiting is going to end. But do not expect much loyalty from what you get. If you try to avoid what you like to get, it will come to you by other ways. You may think that the course you are now taking in your life is a little misleading, but it is not so for this is the right way. You will soon receive startling good news from your best friend. You will also receive rewards for your good service and loyalty.

گفتم غم تو دارم گفتا غمت سر آید / گفتم که ماه من شو گفتا اگر بر آید

گفتم ز مهرورزان رسم وفا بیاموز / گفتا ز خوبرویان این کار کمتر آید

گفتم که بر خیالت راه نظر ببندم / گفتا که شبرو است او از رهِ دیگر آید

گفتم که بوی زلفت گمراه عالَمم کرد / گفتا اگر بدانی هم اوت رهبر آید

گفتم خوشا هوایی کز باد صبح خیزد / گفتا خنک نسیمی کز کوی دلبر آید

گفتم که نوش لعلت ما را به آرزو کشت / گفتا تو بندگی کن کو بنده پرور آید

گفتم دل رحیمت کی عزم صلح دارد / گفتا مگوی با کس تا وقت آن در آید

گفتم زمان عشرت دیدی که چون سر آمد / گفتا خموش حافظ کاین غصه هم سر آید

I have a plan—if I succeed—of course,
To end my trouble, worry and remorse.

The sanctuary of heart isn't fit for the foe,
When angels step in, demons will go.

Why at cruel master's door, one should await,
Long hours for him to appear at the gate.

The good and bad, their merchandise expose,
What really matters is your choice, I suppose.

O' nightingale! Better days you will see;
In green garden again, roses will be.

No wonder that Hafiz is sick and sore,
One who enters tavern, is sober no more.

INTERPRETATION

You are planning to end your sufferings. You will succeed to do so, for your success will bring you great happiness and will automatically end all your troubles. You will find different proposals are put before you for certain matters you have in hand; but what matters is your choice. You should be very careful in your choice and select what befits you. Cheer up, you will soon see much better days and will experience new favorable circumstances.

بر سر آنم که گر ز دست برآید / دست بکاری زنم که غصه سر آید

خلوت دل نیست جای صحبت اضداد / دیو چو بیرون رود فرشته درآید

صحبت حکام ظلمت شب یلداست / نور ز خورشید جوی بو که برآید

بر در ارباب بی مروت دنیا / چند نشینی که خواجه کی بدرآید

ترک گدایی مکن که گنج بیابی / از نظر رهروی که در گذر آید

صالح و طالح متاع خویش نمودند / تا که قبول افتد و که در نظر آید

بلبل عاشق تو عمر خواه که آخر / باغ شود سبز و شاخ گل برآید

غفلت حافظ درین سراچه عجب نیست / هر که به میخانه رفت بی خبر آید

If that heavenly bird, enters my door;
Sweet memories my old head would score.

I hope my tears falling like heavy rain,
The past thunder of wealth, bring back again.

I follow her, I swear to all friends dear;
My corpse won't be back; my news you'll hear.

I will throw my dear soul under her feet,
What else I give when my beauty I meet?

The drum of joy with excitement I beat,
My travelling Moon's back; I desire her to meet.

If not disturbed by guitar and morning sleep,
Beacuse of my prayers her promise 'll keep.

Hafiz expects that her sweet moon-face,
May visit and brighten his gloomy place.

INTERPRETATION

You expect a very dear friend to visit you and to refresh your sweet past memories. You expect that this visit will bring you lots of happiness and worldly privileges. You have decided to follow him or her and to be steadfast in the way he or she puts ahead of you. This will soon happen, and you will feel very exalted and happy. It will bring you lots of new opportunities and successes.

غزلیات حافظ

اگر آن طایر قدسی ز درم باز آید / عمر بگذشته به پیرانه سرم باز آید

دارم امید بر این اشک چو باران که دگر / برق دولت که برفت از نظرم باز آید

آنکه تاج سر من خاک کف پایش بود / از خدا می طلبم تا به سرم باز آید

خواهم اندر عقبش رفت به یاران عزیز / شخصم ار باز نیاید خبرم باز آید

گر نثار قدم یار گرامی نکنم / گو هر جان بچه کار دگرم باز آید

کوس نو دولتی از بام سعادت بزنم / گر ببینم که مه نو سفرم باز آید

مانش ظلفل بچست وشکر خواب صبح / ور نگر بشنود آه سحرم باز آید

آرزومند رخ شاه چو ماهم حافظ / همتی تا به سلامت ز درم باز آید

171

Good news ! Spring came and buds opened;
My pension on wine and flowers I'll spend.

"Where's the wine?" the singing birds all say.
Nightingale says "Who took rose-veil away?"

What does paradise-fruit mean, O'my boy?
But the apple of her chin that I enjoy?

Suffer sorrows since in your quest for gain,
No riches come without suffering pain.

From the moon-faced Saki, take kiss today,
Now that violets all along the garden lay.

Saki's oglings took all my wits away,
So I have no desire, one word to say.

I want to burn this smeared cloak of mine;
The Sage won't take it for a cup of wine.

The Spring passes soon, my wiseman, awake!
The Spring passed by—Hafiz wine did not take.

INTERPRETATION

Be happy, for you are now starting to get results of your past efforts and deeds. This gives you good reason to enjoy your success the best way. Meantime, bear in mind that unless you work hard and suffer ordeals, the great opportunity will not come to you. So, your success will be proportionate to your efforts.

Now that the world turns to your desire, never spend your moments in sadness and worries. But every thing passes quickly and so does your great opportunity—make the most of it.

172

رسید مژده که آمد بهار و سبزه دمید   وظیفه گر برسد مصرفش گل است و نبید

صفیر مرغ برآمد بط شراب کجاست   فغان فتاد و بلبل نقاب گل که کشید

زمینهای بهشتی چه ذوق دریاب   هر آنکه سیب زنخدان شاهدی نگزید

مکن ز غصه شکایت که در طریق طلب   براحتی نرسید آنکه زحمتی نکشید

ز روی ساقی مهوش گلی بچین امروز   که گرد عارض بستان خط بنفشه دمید

چنان کرشمه ساقی دلم ز دست ببرد   که با کسی دگرم نیست برگ گفت و شنید

من این مرقع رنگین چو گل بخواهم سوخت   که پیر باده فروش جرعه نخرید

بهار میگذرد داد و گسترا دریاب

که رفت موسم و حافظ هنوز می نچشید

The Spring cloud appeared with New Year Breeze;
Wine and music need money–how can I seize?

I 'm ashamed of my purse when beauties appear,
Love and poverty are heavy burdens to bear.

People are mean; don't put prestige at stake,
Pawn your cloak and wine and flowers take.

Perhaps my fortune will bring me success;
Since till dawn I prayed, I frankly confess.

With happy smiles the rose to the garden came,
To friend's fragrance they really owe their name.

If my libertine skirt's slitted; no blame.
I wore off a cloak too in piety and fame.

No one described your ruby lips like me,
Though your injustice to me no one can see.

Hafiz received a fatal blow to the heart,
Blood drips of his verse because of love-dart.

INTERPRETATION

*An entirely new era of your career will begin. Things will change
to your favor. You are short of fund, it is true, but be sure you have
a very lucky star and with no money you will make a good success.
You will get great credit soon. Never mind your lack of funds.*

174

ابر آذاری برآمد باد نوروزی وزید   وجه می‌می‌خواهم و مطرب که میگوید برسید

شاهدان در جلوه و من شرمسار کیسه‌ام   بار عشق و مفلسی صعب است می‌باید کشید

قحط جود است آبروی خود نمی‌باید فروخت   باده و گل از بهای خرقه می‌باید خرید

گوییا خواهد گشود از دولتم کاری که دوش   من همی کردم دعا و صبح صادق می‌دمید

بلبلی و صد هزاران خنده زد بر گل بباغ   از گریبان گوییا در گوشه‌اش بویی شنید

دامنی گر چاک شد در عالم رندی چه باک   جامه در نیکنامی نیز می‌باید درید

این لطایف کز لب لعل تو من گفتم که گفت   وین تطاول کز سر زلف تو من دیدم که دید

عدل سلطان گر نپرسد حال مظلومان عشق   گوشه گیران از آسایش طمع باید برید

تیر عاشق کش ندانم بر دل حافظ که زد   این قدر دانم که از شعر ترش خون می‌چکید

175

Come, the victorious flag of Spring appeared,
Of this news both the Sun and Moon have cheered.

Fortune mysteriously unveiled its face;
Tell the oppressed, justice they will embrace.

My Moon appeared! The globe will joyfully spin;
Spring is come; new life will soon begin.

Relate my troubles O' Zephyr, by chance;
Explain my burning heart and my romance.

I have suffered so much hoping her face,
As straw I burn in fire of her disgrace.

Don't sleep Hafiz, for in mansion of grace,
Midnight reveries provide you a place.

INTERPRETATION

A great victory is expected for you. This victory will bring you great credit and happiness. Great fortune will come to you from a source yet undiscovered to you. A new era of success and happiness is approaching you. This will change your life entirely to a better and higher level. This comes to you at a time when you are worn out with hard work and toil and when you are disappointed of ever getting any success.

Now is the time for serious consideration of the problems of your life and for enjoying the fruits of your successes.

بیا که رایت منصور پادشاه رسید   نوید فتح و بشارت بمهر و ماه رسید

جمال بخت ز روی ظفر نقاب انداخت   کمال عدل بفریاد دادخواه رسید

سپهر دور خوش اکنون کند که ماه آمد   جهان بکام دل اکنون رسد که شاه رسید

ز قاطعان طریقی این زمان شود ایمن   قوافل دل و دانش که مرد راه رسید

عزیز مصر برغم برادران غیور   ز قعر چاه بر آمد بأوج ماه رسید

کجاست صوفی دجال فعل ملحد شکل   بگو بسوز که مهدی دین پناه رسید

صبا بگو که چها بر سرم درین غم عشق   ز آتش دل سوزان و دود آه رسید

ز شوق روی تو شاها بدین اسیر فراق   همان رسید کز آتش ببرگ کاه رسید

مرو بخواب که حافظ بپارگاه قبول   ز ورد نیم شب و درس صبحگاه رسید

I forget myself when your beauty display,
The ashes of your victims the wind takes away.

The storm of misfortune ruin 'll bring,
The flood of death will destroy every thing.

Her perfumed curls no one can withstand,
O'vain-hoping heart! Give up this demand.

The glow of my heart exceeded fire-temple's flame,
The tears of my eyes put Tigris to shame.

Ignore opposition; help the Sage enjoy fame,
It doesn't matter if men forget my name.

No gain comes without suffering a pain,
If you seek reward, loyal always remain.

Be kind to me on the day I pass away;
So that forever with peace in grave I stay.

"My long lashes," she said, "Kill you I bet",
O'Lord, help my darling, cruelty forget.

Hafiz, in good temper she won't remain,
Forget her door, stop crying of pain.

INTERPRETATION

In search of your goal you have forgotten yourself and fear no risks. You must expect the hardest temptations in your forthcoming days. Sometimes you wonder whether it is worth to run so much risk. But remember that no gain comes without pain, and so only by suffering all these you have a chance of getting a very high reward. So keep on working with your best energy and the reward will come to you, though it will be for some short time.

روی بنمای و وجود خودم از یاد ببر   خرمن سوختگان را همه گو باد ببر

ما چو دادیم دل و دیده به طوفان بلا   گو بیا سیل غم و خانه ز بنیاد ببر

زلف چون عنبر خامش که ببوید همه بادا   ای دل خام طمع این سخن از یاد ببر

سینه گو شعلهٔ آتشکدهٔ فارس بکش   دیده گو آب رخ دجلهٔ بغداد ببر

دولت پیر مغان باد که باقی سهلست   دیگری گو برو و نام من از یاد ببر

سعی نابرده درین راه بجائی نرسی   مزد اگر می طلبی طاعت استاد ببر

روزِ مرگم نفسی وعدهٔ دیدار بده   وانگهم تا به لحد فارغ و آزاد ببر

دوش میگفت بمژگان درازت بکشم   یا رب از خاطرش اندیشهٔ بیداد ببر

حافظ اندیشه کن از نازکی خاطر یار

برو از درگهش این ناله و فریاد ببر

179

I wish to live and visit tavern again;
All life the servitor of carousels I remain.

Happy is the day when with tears I pass away,
While at tavern door I am happy and gay.

O'Lord, my knowledge all these people resent,
My jewel of truth to others I must present.

My friend may his old companion forsake;
Yet another friend I will never take.

If the Blue Dome would turn to my desire,
Her beloved company I would aspire.

I seek security but this I can't get,
Her enchanting oglings and curls won't let.

Let me tell you, how my secrets unfold,
With lyre and flute at all corners are told.

Hafiz alone isn't in love I say,
Drowned in her love-sea are many this way.

INTERPRETATION

*Your great desire is to get your utopia. You find that your wealth
of knowledge and experience is not well received by those around you.
You look for the day when you will get what you desire. Many people
are deeply involved like you; you are not the only one, so never mind
and keep on working hard and enjoying yourself in the meantime.*

180

گر بود عمر به میخانه رسم بار دگر / بجز از خدمت رندان نکنم کار دگر

خرم آن روز که با دیده گریان بروم / تا زنم آب در میکده یک با ر دگر

معرفت نیست درین قوم خدا را سببی / تا برم گوهر خود در انجمن یار دگر

یار اگر رفت و حق صحبت دیرین نشناخت / حاش لله که روم من ز پی یار دگر

گر مساعد شود م دایره چشم کبود / هم به دست آورمش باز به پرگار دگر

عافیت می طلبد خاطرم از بیگذارند / غمزه شوخش و آن طره طرار دگر

راز سر بسته ما بین که به دستان گفتند / هر زمان با دف و نی بر سر بازار دگر

هر دم از درد بنالم که فلک هر ساعت / کند م قصد دل ریش به آزار دگر

Joseph will come back to Canaan again,
My house the fragrance of her rose-garden will regain.

O sad heart, from hardships do not get mad,
Your worries will soon end— don't feel so sad.

If the Spring on turf-throne would remain,
The bird under flower-canopy sits again .

If the world turns to your favor some days,
Take it easy; it won't do so always.

If God's secrets are unknown don't despair.
Behind the mystery-curtain is a love-affair.

O'Heart, if death-flood sweeps off all life,
Your pilot as Noah, ends your strife.

When through desert you pass for pilgrimage,
If thorns bother your feet, don't be in rage.

The road 's perilous and destination away.
Yet all roads have their ends, I daresay.

Enemies oppose me in absence of friend,
God knows that on Him I only depend .

Hafiz, the dark, lonely nights never mind,
Study and pray—thus salvation you find.

INTERPRETATION

You have a friend far away whom you have not seen or heard of for a long time. He is coming back to you soon with lots of joy and new opportunities. This will help you to solve many of your problems and difficulties. But remember that in order to get what you ultimately desire, you must suffer hardships. The course you take is perilous, but if you endure these perils, there is certainty for your success. After some dark days , the twilight of your success will appear, and you will be enjoying a long period of happiness.

یوسف گم گشته بازآید به کنعان غم مخور   کلبه احزان شود روزی گلستان غم مخور

ای دل غمدیده حالت به شود دل بد مکن   وین سر شوریده بازآید به سامان غم مخور

گر بهار عمر باشد باز بر تخت چمن   چتر گل در سر کشی ای مرغ خوشخوان غم مخور

دور گردون گر دو روزی بر مراد ما نرفت   دائماً یکسان نباشد حال دوران غم مخور

هان مشو نومید چون واقف نه‌ای از سر غیب   باشد اندر پرده بازیهای پنهان غم مخور

ای دل ار سیل فنا بنیاد هستی برکند   چون ترا نوح است کشتیبان ز طوفان غم مخور

در بیابان گر به شوق کعبه خواهی زد قدم   سرزنشها گر کند خار مغیلان غم مخور

گر چه منزل بس خطرناک است و مقصد بس بعید   هیچ راهی نیست کانرا نیست پایان غم مخور

حال ما در فرقت جانان و ابرام رقیب   جمله میداند خدای حال گردان غم مخور

حافظا در کنج فقر و خلوت شبهای تار   تا بود وردت دعا و درس قرآن غم مخور

183

I give you my advice, hearken and obey,
Hear your friend's advice, without delay.

Make the most of your youth, while you can,
For old time is in ambush, my young man.

The two worlds mean nothing to lovers true.
Fun is plenty, but love is rare for you .

I seek good company; let musicians play,
In bass and alto Iyre sentiments display.

If according to my plan, the world spins,
I promise not to drink nor to commit sins.

At eternity in absentia, destinies were made.
Things may be against your will; I am afraid.

Saki! Like lily serve the fragrant wine;
Though of her mole in my memory will shine.

Saki! Serve the wine-cup; it is so pure.
Tell the jealous Sheikh, we are secure.

I repented from wine, but often broke,
When Saki with oglings kind words spoke.

My disillusioned heart, none will receive;
Only the true lovers my state perceive.

Forget repentance Hafiz, at this good time,
Lest Saki's oglings kill you for this crime.

INTERPRETATION

Appreciate your days of youth or old age, whichever it is, for no one knows how long one may live. Stick to true love, which is worth more than fun or pleasure. You will find that all things will not be according to your will and sometimes things may happen against your will. You must take them as they are. You will break your promise against your will several times, but it will be worthwhile for you.

نصیحتی کنت بشنو و بهانه مگیر
هر آنچه ناصح مشفق بگویدت بپذیر

ز وصل روی جوانان تمتعی بردار
که در کمین گه عمر است مکر عالم پیر

نعیم هر دو جهان پیش عاشقان بجوی
که این متاع قلیل است و آن عطای کثیر

معاشری خوش و رودی بساز می‌خواهم
که درد خویش بگویم به ناله‌ی بم و زیر

بر آن سرم که ننوشم می و گنه نکنم
اگر موافق تدبیر من شود تقدیر

چو قسمت ازلی بی حضور ما کردند
گر اندکی نه به وفق رضاست خرده مگیر

چو لاله در قدحم ریز ساقیا می و مشک
که نقش خال نگارم نمی‌رود ز ضمیر

بیار ساغر و در خوشاب ای ساقی
حسود گو کرم آصفی ببین و بمیر

به عزم توبه نهادم قدح ز کف صد بار
ولی کرشمه‌ی ساقی نمی‌کند تقصیر

می دو ساله و محبوب چارده ساله
همین بس است مرا صحبت صغیر و کبیر

دل رمیده‌ی ما را که پیش می‌گیرد
خبر دهید به مجنون خسته از زنجیر

حدیث توبه در این بزمگه مگو حافظ
که ساقیان کمان ابرویت زنند تیر

185

I am not satisfied with your love's bliss;
I drink dregs, hoping ruby lips to kiss.

I lost heart and faith when I saw the friend,
What her friendship will bring me in the end!

Saki! Serve a cup of water with fire;
Though I'm crude in love, her beauty I admire.

The Sun saw in my home your beauty sublime,
Began sneaking on roofs all the time .

Once at random the friend recalled my name,
That's why wisdom brought me such a fame.

At eternity from His lips I sipped wine,
I'm still mellow with the wine divine .

"Give life" she said , "And I'll give you rest."
You won't do that, but I will do my best.

Hafiz, when her ruby lips you explain,
Your pen, then water of life will contain .

INTERPRETATION

You are not satisfied with your existing blessings and expect
greater privileges. You are wondering what will be the result of strife
and efforts. But you will soon have a great privilege that will be envied
by many around you. This will bring you great prestige and honor.

بر نیامد از تمنای لبت کامم هنوز برامید جام لعلت درد ی آشامم هنوز

روز اول رفت دینم در سر زلفین تو تا چه خواهد شد در این سودا سرانجامم هنوز

ساقیا یک جرعه ز آن آب آتشگون که من از خطا گفتم شبی زلف ترا مشک ختن

پرتو روی تو تا در خلوتم دید آفتاب می رود چون سایه هر دم بر در و بامم هنوز

نام من رفتست روزی بر لب جانان بسهو اهل دل را بوی جان می آید از نامم هنوز

در ازل داده ست ما را ساقی لعل لبت جرعه جامی که من مدهوش آن جامم هنوز

ای که گفتی جان بده تا باشدت آرام جان جان بغمهایش سپردم نیست آرامم هنوز

در قلم آورد حافظ قصه لعل لبش
آب حیوان میرود هر دم ز اقلامم هنوز

From the world's garden I desire one rose,
With my cypress at the world-turf to repose.

God forbid that hypocrites I join or admire,
Of all good things of life , the wine I desire .

Paradise palace is reward for your good deed,
For us libertines, tavern will do indeed .

Sit at the brook and watch the march of time.
For, to me this is a destiny sublime.

See what the world gives! Its fun and sorrow;
You may want it, but I don't want tomorrow.

When the friend is with me nothing I seek,
His company makes me strong, though I am weak .

O' Lord! To Hafiz paradise do not offer,
Your sanctuary to all existence I prefer.

Hafiz, if you grumble, you will entice ,
Your versatile poetry for you suffice.

INTERPRETATION

You are somewhat disappointed of your past deeds and expect to get failure rather than success. You want and expect defeat rather than victory. But you should stop expecting evil, for what you have done already deserves a much better reward than what you expect.

گلعذاری زگلستان جهان ما راس

زین چمن سایهٔ آن سرو روان ما راس

من وهمصحبتی اهل ریا دورم باد

از گرانان جهان رطل گران ما راس

قصر فردوس بپاداش عمل می بخشند

ما که رندیم و گدا دیر مغان ما راس

بنشین بر لب جوی و گذر عمر ببین

کاین اشارت ز جهان گذران ما راس

نقد بازار جهان بنگر و آزار جهان

گر شما را نبس این سود و زیان ما راس

یار با ماست چه حاجت که زیادت طلبیم

دولت صحبت آن مونس جان ما راس

از در خویش خدا را به بهشتم مفرست

که سر کوی تو از کون و مکان ما راس

حافظ از مشرب قسمت گله نانصاف است

طبع چون آب و غزلهای روان ما راس

Her black curls account for my great distress;
What a tramp I am, I cannot express!

In hope of loyalty don't give heart and creed ,
On my part I repent for my past deed.

For a drink that causes none a bother ,
I suffer much from ignorants, brother .

O' Sheikh! For ruby wine, Hafiz forgive .
Wine took my faith and heart. Will you believe?

Many problems occupied my soul this way;
"Don't see, don't ask," the clergy always say .

With sanctity I always wish to remain;
Her charming eyes my impiety explain.

I went to consult the revolving-ball,
It said,"God's bat makes me to rise and fall."

I asked, "In whose blood your curls bath'll take?"
She said, "Hafiz, forget this for God's sake.

INTERPRETATION

Don't go too far in your commitments, for you will find that it will be hard to fulfill them. You are already beginning to realise that perhaps you have gone too far in your commitments. You wish you had not gone so far. But remembering the past events, you are justified to have overstepped your limits. You are not the only person who has exceeded his limits. Lots of other persons are also invloved like your self. But somehow, you will escape the evil effects of your excessive action, for which you must be very grateful.

190

دارم از زلف سیاهش گله چندان که مپرس
که چنان زو شده‌ام بی سر و سامان که مپرس

کس بامید وفا ترک دل و دین مکناد
که چنانم من از این کرده پشیمان که مپرس

بیکی جرعه که آزارکسش در پی نیست
زحمتی می‌کشم از مردم نادان که مپرس

زاهد از ما بسلامت بگذر کاین می لعل
دل و دین می‌برد از دست بدان سان که مپرس

گفت و گوهاست درین راه که جان بگدازد
هر کسی عربده این که مبین آن که مپرس

پارسائی و سلامت هوسم بود ولی
شیوه‌ای می‌کند آن نرگس فتان که مپرس

گفتم از گوی فلک صورت حالی پرسم
گفت آن می‌کشم اندر خم چوگان که مپرس

گفتمش زلف بخون که شکستی گفتا
حافظ این قصه دراز است بقرآن که مپرس

By mysterious voice at dawn I was told : -
"A bold king is ruling; drink and be bold."

People of insight nothing will conceal,
New teachings they now give and truths reveal .

With tune of lyre my stories I resume ,
If I keep them in heart, it will consume.

Let us drink wine, before Sheriff appears,
Drink with friends and exchange joyous cheers .

Last night the Sheikh was seen drunk in a crime ,
Though he carried his prayer-rug all the time .

If you seek salvation, then I propose,
Don't be debaucherous, nor your piety expose.

God's grace brings you revelation divine,
To seek God's sanctuary, your soul refine.

Except for God your voice should never raise,
God's eyes and ears friendly messages appraise.

The kings can best determine what they will;
Hafiz— you secluded Dervish —keep still.

INTERPRETATION

Do not be afraid of propagating your beliefs. Since what you believe in, is right, so do not hesitate to propagate it to others. Appreciate the great value of your present opportunities, and enjoy yourself fully. If you seek success, do not try to be shamful, rather be truthful and honest to yourself and to your God. God's grace will soon bring you some great blessings, and you should try to refine yourself in lieu of God's outpouring grace. Your sincerity and honesty will be certainly accounted for .

سحر ز هاتف غیبم رسید مژده بگوش   که دور شاه شجاع است می دلیر بنوش

شد آنکه اهل نظر بر کناره میرفتند   هزار گونه سخن در دهان و لب خاموش

بصوت چنگ بگوییم آن حکایتها   که از نهفتن آن دیگ سینه میزد جوش

شراب خانگی ترس محتسب خورده   بروی یار بنوشیم و بانگ نوشانوش

ز کوی میکده دوشش بدوش میبردند   امام شهر که سجاده میکشید بدوش

دلا دلالت خیرت کنم براه نجات   مکن بفسق مباهات و زهد هم مفروش

محل نور تجلیست رای انور شاه   چو قرب او طلبی در صفای نیت کوش

بجز ثنای جلالش مساز ورد ضمیر   که هست گوش دلش محرم پیام سروش

رموز مصلحت ملک خسروان دانند
گدای گوشه نشینی تو حافظ مخروش

Last night the Sage unfolded secrets great;
I will expose his secrets, any rate: -

"Take things easy for an easy reward .
"The world is hard to those who take it hard."

The Sage passed the cup with a clever blink ,
(The cup made Saturn dance) saying , "Drink".

"This cup has blood within but a smile on face,
"Don't be noisy (like lyre) , for a little disgrace.

"No secrets divulged to those not sincere,
"The angels' secrets the demons won't hear.

"My son, for the mean world never feel sad;
"If you're intelligent, hear this, my lad.

Hafiz's sins are known to the friend ,
Serve wine His mercy will come in the end.

INTERPRETATION

If you seek easy reward, take things easy yourself. If you take things very seriously , the world will also treat you seriously. You may face certain difficulties and inconveniences, but take them easy, and you will succeed. Never feel sad for what is expected to happen, for God will help you soon and you will get his blessings in the end.

دوش با من گفت پنهان کاردانی تیزهوش   وز شما پنهان نشاید کرد سر می فروش

گفت آسان گیر بر خود کارها کز روی طبع   سخت می‌گیرد جهان بر مردمان سخت‌کوش

وانگهم درداد جامی کز فروغش بر فلک   زهره در رقص آمد و بربط‌زنان می‌گفت نوش

با دل خونین لب خندان بیاور همچو جام   نی گرت زخمی رسد آیی چو چنگ اندر خروش

تا نگردی آشنا زین پرده رمزی نشنوی   گوش نامحرم نباشد جای پیغام سروش

گوش کن پند ای پسر وز بهر دنیا غم مخور   گفتمت چون در حدیثی گر توانی داشت گوش

در حریم عشق نتوان زد دم از گفت و شنید   زان که آنجا جمله اعضا چشم باید بود و گوش

بر بساط نکته‌دانان خودفروشی شرط نیست   یا سخن دانسته گو ای مرد عاقل یا خموش

ساقیا می ده که رندیهای حافظ فهم کرد

آصف صاحب‌قران جرم‌بخش عیب‌پوش

My luck in this city I have tried .
No more in this abyss I will abide .

I gnaw my hands much and sigh with regret ,
Like rose, my shattered body I forget .

While the rose gave to the garden a sight ,
The nightingale on rose sang this tonight : -

"Don't worry if she is angry and mad,
"Of her own bad luck is indeed she sad .

"Expect the world to go easy with you ?
"Forget harsh words— to covenants be true."

Being separated from God my heart is sad,
I'll set afire all the fortune I had.

Hafiz! If all were to enjoy success,
Jam would never leave his throne in distress.

INTERPRETATION

You will find that if you travel from your city of residence to another city, things will be a little better for you. Every thing seems against you here. In your new place, you will enjoy better living and better opportunities. The world will go easy with you in your new place. But of course, in your new city, you will always feel homesick and desire to go back to your old place.

ما آزموده‌ایم در این شهر بخت خویش   بیرون کشید باید از این ورطه رخت خویش

از بس که دست میگزم و آب میکشم   آتش زدم چو گل به تن سخت سخت خویش

دوشم ز بلبلی چه خوش آمد که می‌سرود   گل گوش پهن کرده ز شاخ درخت خویش

کای دل تو شاد باش که آن یار تندخو   بسیار تندروی نشیند ز بخت خویش

خواهی که سخت و سست جهان بر تو بگذرد   بگذر ز عهد سست و سخنهای سخت خویش

وقت است کز فراق تو و ز سوز اندرون   آتش در افکنم به همه رخت و بخت خویش

ای حافظ ار مراد میسر شدی مدام   جمشید نیز هم به رها نمودی تخت خویش

I'll get her skirt, if luck is on my side,
Joyfully I seek her, cunningly she'll hide.

My hopeful heart saw loyalty from none.
Though my love-story everywhere 's gone.

The curve of your eyebrow calamity brought;
Precious life wasted in unhappy thought.

If her eyebrow in my dream would appear,
No target misses, even in dream , I fear.

Love of hard-hearted beauties I expect ,
Bad boys pay their old father no respect .

I plan to forget love and to retire,
But musicians will beat me with their lyre.

The Sheikhs with incantations silence command;
Sheriff is drunk with sham; wine I demand.

Hafiz, if to the road of truth you resort ,
The saints' goodwill your life journey 'll escort.

INTERPRETATION

*Be happy, for you will finally succeed to get what you desire.
Sometimes you will feel your aim is out of sight; other times you will
see it very near you. But finally you will get it. If you keep up with high
standards and always be honest and truthful, you will always be
successful.*

198

طالع اگر مدد دهد دامنش آورم بکف / گر بکشم زهی طرب ور بکشد زهی شرف

طرف کرم ز کس نبست این دل پرامید من / گر چه سخن همی برد قصه من بهر طرف

از غم ابروی توام هیچ گشایشی نشد / وه که درین خیال کج عمر عزیز شد تلف

ابروی دوست کی شود دست کش خیال من / کس نزد است ازین کمان تیر مرا به هدف

چند به ناز پرورم مهر بتان سنگدل / یاد پدر نمیکنند این پسران ناخلف

من به خیال زاهدی گوشه نشین و طرفه آنک / مغبچه زهر طرف میزند به چنگ دف

بی خبرند زاهدان نقش بخوان و لا تقل / مست ریاست محتسب باده بده و لا تخف

صوفی شهر بین که چون لقمه شبهه میخورد / پاردمش دراز باد آن حیوان خوش علف

حافظ اگر قدم زنی در ره خاندان بصدق
بدرقه رهت شود همت شحنه نجف

A secure place, intimate friend 'n' pure wine,
If you always get, it's really fine.

The world-bliss is vague if you well look,
Tedious studies on this subject I undertook .

How fortunate! Till now I didn't comprehend,
Nothing is as dear as a friend— a friend !

Find a remote place and yourself enjoy,
The world is in ambush, your life 'll destroy.

Come! repent, her lips and wine forget ,
Wisdom such repentance condemns, I bet.

The apple of her chin is attractive and sweet ,
The careful thoughts of men, its depth can't reach.

She said "Hafiz, I like your fluent rhyme,"
I am sure she is fooling me this time .

INTERPRETATION

One of the things you have so far put little emphasis on, is the importance of a good friend. A friend may change the whole course of your life. His good or bad habits easily affect you. So you must be very careful about the friends around you and enjoy the company of the best of them. If you select good friends, you are going to have a very thriving career, and will enjoy lots of blessings. So study the friends around you once more and reconsider some of them.

200

مقام امن و می بی‌غش و رفیق شفیق
گرت مدام میسر شود زهی توفیق

جهان و کار جهان جمله هیچ بر هیچ است
هزار بار من این نکته کرده‌ام تحقیق

دریغ و درد که تا این زمان ندانستم
که کیمیای سعادت رفیق بود رفیق

بیا منی رو و فرصت شمر غنیمت وقت
که در کمین که مرزند قاطعان طریق

بیا که توبه ز لعل نگار و خنده جام
حکایتی است که عقلش نمی‌کند تصدیق

اگر چه موی میانت به چون منی نرسد
خوش است خاطرم از گر این خیال دقیق

حلاوتی که ترا در چه زنخدان است
بکنه آن نرسد صد هزار فکر عمیق

اگر برنگ عقیقی شد اشک من چه عجب
که مهر خاتم لعل تو هست همچو عقیق

بخنده گفت که حافظ غلام طبع توام
ببین که تا به چه حدم همی کند تحمیق

When you drink wine, spill some on the clay,
Let by this sin, someone benefit some day.

Be content with what you have - say no word;
Time ruthlessly kills souls with its sword.

In paradise or hell, for man or jin,
Being a miser is considered a sin .

The Grave-Architect, has closed to us the way,
So there's no exit for us from under clay.

The charm of wine has so misled the sane,
That all his life in vineyard will remain.

On the tavern-road Hafiz will pass away,
O'clean-hearted man, for his clean heart pray.

INTERPRETATION

Let other people benefit from the blessings you have in your life. Be content with all the great blessings you have and be sure you are one of the lucky souls. Be a little more generous in your spending, and spend some of your money for good and benevolent causes. As we know, there is no escape from death, and so the wealth we accumulate must be spent for the good of mankind. So, enjoy yourself with the resources you have and alot some part of it to charity and benevolent purposes.

اگر شراب خوری جرعه‌ای فشان بر خاک   از آن گناه که نفعی رسد بغیر چه باک

برو بهر چه تو داری بخور دریغ مخور   که بی دریغ زند روزگار تیغ هلاک

بخاک پای تو ای سرو نازپرور من   که روز واقعه پا وامگیرم از سر خاک

چه دوزخی چه بهشتی چه آدمی چه پری   بمذهب همه کفر طریقت است امساک

مهندس فلکی راه دیر شش جهتی   چنان ببست که ره نیست زیر دیر مغاک

فریب دختر رز طرفه میزند ره عقل   مباد تا بقیامت خراب طارم تاک

برو بمیکده حافظ خوش از جهان بگذر

دعای اهل دلت باد مونس دل پاک

Enemies an attempt against my life may dare;
If you're a friend, enemies I do not care
I'm happy with hope of meeting the friend,
His separation will bring my life to end.

If her news from Zephyr I do not hear,
Like the roses all my garments I tear.

With your thoughts my eyes continue to weep;
When separated I cannot enjoy sleep

Your tyrannies I prefer to others' balm;
Even your poison, as cure, 'll make me calm.

No need to kill me with a sharp sword,
I surrender my soul - just say a word!

If you kill me with a sword I'll yield -
Only my head and heart will be my shield.

What God is, no human eye can ever see.
Every one judges him according to capacity.

In the eyes of people Hafiz is dear ,
When in need at your door, nothing I fear.

INTERPRETATION

You may face much opposition from your friends, but they won't be able to do you any serious harm, if you trust the Lord. You feel very impatient to get what you desire, but if you fully trust the Lord and move by his guiding light and inspiration, you should fear nothing.

هزار دشمنم ار میکنند قصد هلاک   گرم تو دوستی از دشمنان ندارم باک

مرا امید وصال تو زنده میدارد   وگرنه هر دمم از هجر تست بیم هلاک

نفس نفس اگر از باد نشنوم بویش   زمان زمان چو گل از غم کنم گریبان چاک

رود بخواب دو چشم از خیال تو هیهات   بود صبور دل اندر فراق تو حاشاک

اگر تو زخم زنی به که دیگری مرهم   وگر تو زهر دهی به که دیگری تریاک

بضرب سیفک قتلی حیاتنا ابدا   لان روحی قد طاب ان یکون فداک

عنان مپیچ که گر میزنی بشمشیرم   سپر کنم سر و دستت ندارم از فتراک

ترا چنانکه تویی هر نظر کجا بیند   بقدر دانش خود هر کسی کند ادراک

بچشم خلق عزیز جهان شود حافظ

که بر در تو نهد روی مسکنت بر خاک

205

No matter how I define, my beautiful girl,
When people heard me said "She's a pearl:"

Love and libertinism first easy I took,
To get these virtues many troubles I brook.

Hallaj on the gallows truth did reveal,
But religious leaders such truth conceal.

"When my soul" I asked, "Your company'll gain?"
She said"When life no obstacle'll remain."

To a cunning beauty I give my heart,
She's fine qualities and yet is very smart.

Secluded Hafiz– like your eyes mellow goes,
He follows the drunk, like your eyebrows.

Hafiz saves you from evils of all kind,
I dream my hands around her neck to find.

INTERPRETATION

*The way of love is the hardest way, and yet you thought this wa
the easiest road to walk into. It is a long and tedious journey.*

*You seem to ignore the great personal power and influence you
have over things. Exercise your personal power and influence and
things will move in your direction more favorably. You will be protected from many evils.*

هر نکته‌ای که گفتم در وصف آن شمایل   هر کو شنید گفتا لله در قائل

تحصیل عشق و رندی آسان نمود اول   آخر بسوخت جانم در کسب این فضائل

حلاج بر سر دار این نکته خوش سراید   از شافعی نپرسند امثال این مسائل

گفتم که کی ببخشی بر جان ناتوانم   گفت آن زمان که نبود جان در میان حائل

دل داده‌ام بیاری شوخی کشی نگاری   مرضیه السجایا محموده الخصائل

در عین گوشه گیری بودم چو چشم مستت   واکنون شدم به مستان چون ابروی تو مائل

از آب دیده صد ره طوفان نوح دیدم   وز لوح سینه نقشت هرگز نگشت زائل

ای دوست دست حافظ تعویذ چشم زخمست

یا رب ببینم آنرا در گردنت حمائل

Except putting heart and wisdom at stake,
What benefit from your love could I take?

Your love exposed my life-crop to the wind,
Be sure your covenant I wouldn't rescind.

Though a meagre particle, I'm deep in love,
Searching your face, went to Heaven above.

Serve wine, since not one moment of my life,
I was destined to be free of strife.

O' admonitor, if you are sober, I say;
"Don't waste your efforts, I'm drunk today."

Before my friend I am really ashamed,
I can't serve him, but I'm not to be blamed.

Hafiz consumed and his friend didn't say,
"I'll remedy harms done to you, any way."

INTERPRETATION

You may think that you have put too much at stake for your heart's desire. It may be true, but you are still consistent in your aim. This great devotion, however, will lift you up and bring you good luck. So cheer up!

غزلیات حافظ

بیزار از آنکه بشد دین و دانش از دستم | بیا بگو که ز مشتت چه طرف بربستم

اگر چه خرمن عمرم غم تو داد به باد | بخاک پای عزیزت که عهد نشکستم

چو از ره آمدی ای دولت مشتاق | که در هوای رخت چون سبوبر پوستم

بیا رباده که عمر بیت تا من از سر آن | بکنج عافیت از بهر عیش ننشستم

اگر ز مردم هشیاری ای نصیحت گو | سخن بخاک میفکن چرا که من مستم

چگونه سر ز خجالت برآورم بر دوست | که خدمتی بسزا برنیامد از دستم

بسوخت حافظ و آن یار دلنواز نگفت
که مرهمی بفرستم که خاطرش خستم

209

Openly I announce, happily declare: -
Captive of love, for the two worlds I don't care.

I was bird of paradise, I can't explain,
How was cast out to this snare of pain.

In paradise garden I lived as angel,
Adam brought me down to this earthly Hell.

Paradise beauties, its garden and its pool,
I give up for God's sake, I'm not a fool.

On my heart-leaf is recorded the friend;
My master taught nothing else to the end.

No astrologer knew the star of my fate,
Such an unhappy birth, O.'Lord, I hate.

The slave of love-tavern I've become,
Every moment new troubles I welcome.

If my eye drinks heart-blood do not wonder,
For I left heart to her ruthless plunder.

With your hair wipe from Hafiz's eyes his blood,
Or he 'll be drowned in this overwhelming flood.

INTERPRETATION

*If you are a captive of love, then you do not care for anything
in this world—nor for the next world.*

*You seem to have enjoyed a great reputation for high standards,
but now have degraded. Have given up all your privileges because
you are attached to certain pleasures. Few people in this world have
had the unexpected downfall that you have so far had. This downfall
has brought you new problems and difficulties. But there will soon be
a remedy to all your troubles and misfortunes, and fortune will wipe
off your tearful eyes and lead you to a better life.*

فاش می‌گویم و از گفتهٔ خود دلشادم   بندهٔ عشقم و از هر دو جهان آزادم

طایر گلشن قدسم چه دهم شرح فراق   که درین دامگه حادثه چون افتادم

من ملک بودم و فردوس برین جایم بود   آدم آورد درین دیر خراب آبادم

سایهٔ طوبی و دلجوئی حور و لب حوض   بهوای سر کوی تو برفت از یادم

نیست بر لوح دلم جز الف قامت دوست   چکنم حرف دگر یاد نداد استادم

کوکب بخت مرا هیچ منجم نشناخت   یا رب از مادر گیتی بچه طالع زادم

تا شدم حلقه بگوش در میخانهٔ عشق   هر دم آید غمی از نو بمبارکبادم

می‌خورد خون دلم مردمک دیده سزاست   که چرا دل بجگر گوشهٔ مردم دادم

پاک کن چهرهٔ حافظ بسر زلف ز اشک   ور نه این سیل دمادم ببرد بنیادم

211

In flood of tears last night, tried to sleep,
But her memory drowned me in my tears deep.

I thought of your brows, my heart went ablaze,
To see your beauty, deep in cup I gaze.

The friend has appeared with a face so bright,
In ecstacy I sent kisses to the moonlight.

My eyes fixed to Saki—my ears to the harp -
Expecting augury, ears and eyes were sharp.

Till twilight I kept thinking of her face,
To my restless eyes I promised her grace.

Saki! Served wine by the tune of this ode;
While I made verses at the Sage's abode.

Hafiz! You have good time; get your desire,
In memory of the friend, joyfully, retire.

INTERPRETATION

You have some worries inside you that have taken all rest and happiness away from you. In search of your heart's desire you are working very hard, and with all your might. Every moment you expect the unexpected to happen, and your heart's desire to come true. Cheer up and have great joy, for you will soon have it, and this will make your life so much brighter and more meaningful. The rest of your life will be full of happy days, for you have got what you were after, and this great blessing will be appreciated by you all through your life.

دوش بی سیل اشکم ره خواب می‌زدم   نقشی به یاد خط تو بر آب می‌زدم

ابروی یار در نظر و خرقه سوخته   جامی به یاد گوشه محراب می‌زدم

هر مرغ فکر کز سر شاخ سخن بجست   باز ش ز طره تو به مضراب می‌زدم

روی نگار در نظرم جلوه می‌نمود   وز دور بوسه بر رخ مهتاب می‌زدم

چشم بر روی ساقی و گوشم به قول   فالی به چشم و گوش در این باب می‌زدم

نقش خیال روی تو تا وقت صبحدم   بر کارگاه دیده بی خواب می‌زدم

ساقی به صوت این غزلم کاسه می‌گرفت   می‌گفتم این سرود و می ناب می‌زدم

خوش بود وقت حافظ و فال مراد و کام

بر نام عمر و دولت احباب می‌زدم

Though I am old, weak and in disgrace,
I get young when I think of your fine face.

Thank God, whatever from him I request,
I'm always successful in my good quest.

My world flower! Enjoy glory and fame,
In world-garden your nightingale I became.

I was ignorant of the world's fall and rise,
In your love-school I have become so wise.

Destiny ordered me at tavern to stay,
Destiny's orders we all have to obéy.

Wisdom-gate was opened to me, behold!
While I resided at the Sage's threshold.

In eternal bliss I sit high on throne,
Cup-in-hand, of friend's grace, I'm prone.

I'm not old,but loyal is not my friend,
When I reach her my life will come to end.

Last night grace gave me good news to say,
"Hafiz, your sins are forgiven today."

INTERPRETATION

Though you may be tired and worn-out of troublesome events of the past, yet the memory of your future successes gives you fresh energy and a dynamic power. You are certain of your ultimate victory. For this reason you are very happy and uplifted. Great joy and great blessings will soon pour on you, and you will enjoy the greatest successes all through the rest of your life. God's grace and forgiveness will also come to you in plenty.

هرچند پیر و خسته دل و ناتوان شدم   هرگز که یاد روی تو کردم جوان شدم

شکر خدا که هر چه طلب کردم از خدا   بر منتهای همت خود کامران شدم

ای گلبن جوان بر دولت بجز که من   در سایهٔ تو بلبل باغ جهان شدم

اول ز تخت و فوق وجودم خبر نبود   در مکتب غم تو چنین نکته دان شدم

قسمت حوالتم بجز اینها میکند   هرچند کاندرین شدم و آنچنان شدم

آن روز بر دلم در معنی گشوده شد   کز ساکنان درگه پیر مغان شدم

در شاهراه دولت سرمد به تخت بخت   با جام می   بکام دل دوستان شدم

از آنزمان که فتنهٔ چشمت بمن رسید   ایمن ز شر فتنهٔ آخر زمان شدم

من پیر سال و ماه نیم یار بیوفاست   بر من چو عمر میگذرد پیر از آن شدم

دوشم نوید داد عنایت که حافظا   باز آ که من بعفو گناهت ضمان شدم

215

Smiling face and charming locks I desire,
Languishing eyes–and wine with some fire !

Eternity's secret let me express :-
Only when wine removes my distress.

I am paradise Adam, but on this trip,
I love charming beauty and ruby lip.

In love we must suffer, smile 'n' admire,
As candles we stand fearless of fire.

Shiraz's full of ruby lips, and eyes black,
Being a poor jeweller, such fortunes I lack.

Many languishing eyes in Shiraz I see,
Even without the wine, mellow I can be.

Shiraz is full of beauties short and tall,
I've no money, otherwise I want them all.

If fortune helps me to reach my friend,
Meaning of happiness I would comprenend.

Hafiz, your talent in beauties display;
But finding none, you sigh in great dismay.

INTERPRETATION

You feel now that your past life has been a bit dull and that you have not had any real fun. You will go on a long trip, and this will change the direction of your tastes, likes and dislikes. This journey will bring to you lots of new opportunities and new aspirations, all of which you will not be able to achieve naturally. But being of a greedy frame of mind, you desire to get them all. If you get your main desire, the rest will follow, so strive hard towards your original goal, and do not go astray.

من دوستدار روی خوش و موی دلکشم
مدهوش چشم مست و می صاف بی‌غشم

گفتی ز سرّ عهد ازل یک سخن بگو
آنگه کنم بیان که دو پیمانه درکشم

من آدم بهشتیم اما درین سفر
حالی اسیر عشق جوانان مه‌وشم

در عاشقی گزیر نباشد ز ساز و سوز
استاده‌ام چو شمع مترسان ز آتشم

شیراز معدن لب لعلست و کان حسن
من جوهری مفلسم ایرا مشوشم

از بس که چشم مست درین شهر دیده‌ام
حقا که می نمی‌خورم اکنون و سرخوشم

شهریست پر کرشمه حوران ز شش جهت
چیزیم نیست ورنه خریدار هر ششم

بختا ز مدّه دو که کشم زحمتی ز دوست
گیسوی حور گر فشاند زنم غرشم

حافظ عروس طبع مرا جلوه آرزوست
آیینه‌ای ندارم از آن آه می‌کشم

٢١٧

Like wine-barrel I cinder from inside,
But seal my lips, drink blood and agony hide.

If you covet her lips, yourself you kill;
Attempts against my life I make still.

When my heart will be from all sorrow-free?
Those black curls of her really enslave me.

God forbid that myself, pious I think,
Though once a while only a cup I drink.

With all my sins on judgement day, I believe,
God's eternal grace I'll also receive.

Adam for two barleys sold the paradise-
I'm not Adam's son if I do otherwise.

My cloak of sham piety does not reveal,
My hidden defects thereunder I conceal.

I would rather drink from the barrel's edge,
If my Sage considers this a privilege.

If singers continue love-song to sing;
The odes of Hafiz happiness will bring.

INTERPRETATION

Some great trouble is now worrying you. But you keep quiet and hide your troubles from people. You realise that what you are after involves some dangers, but you still do it, not fearing any thing. It will take a long time for you to fight on your way, but success will come to you in the end. This success will bring you lots of opportunities and new privileges. But you will get rid of these too, soon. If you try hard again, there is a chance of another success for you, which you should hold fast to this time and fully enjoy.

من که از آتش دل چون خم می در جوشم   مهر بر لب زده خون می‌خورم و خاموشم

قصد جانست طمع در لب جانان کردن   تو مرا بین که در این کار به جان می‌کوشم

من کی آزاد شوم از غم دل چون بروم   هندوی زلف بتی حلقه کند در گوشم

حاش لله که نه‌ام معتقد طاعت خویش   این قدر هست که گه گه قدحی می‌نوشم

هست امیدم که علی رغم عدو روز جزا   فیض عفوش ننهد بار گنه بر دوشم

پدرم روضه رضوان به دو گندم بفروخت   من چرا ملک جهان را به جوی نفروشم

خرقه پوشی من از غایت دین داری نیست   پرده‌ای بر سر صد عیب نهان می‌پوشم

من که خواهم که ننوشم بجز از راوق خم   چکنم گر سخن پیر مغان ننیوشم

گر از این دست زند مطرب مجلس ره عشق
شعر حافظ ببرد وقت سماع از هوشم

I'm no libertine if from love 'n' wine repent;
Sheriff knows such repentance I resent.

I objected to those who repentance had,
If I repent from Spring-wine, I'm mad.

Love is a pearl, tavern sea— there I dive.
Never mind if from this sea won't come alive.

On firmament's covenant one can't rely,
A covenant with wine-cup you better try.

Though a beggar, I have a treasure rare,
For the revolvings of mean world I don't care.

If my merciful friend gave me Hell fire,
How mean of me—paradise brooks to desire!

Last night her ruby lips brought me relief,
Yet in her loyalty I have no belief.

INTERPRETATION

You may have decided many times to abstain from certain things, but you have not done so. You are now emerging deep into a perilous adventure. You will face many dangers; but you will gain great privi - leges too. You will get lots of credit and respect for your adventures, when you come out safely, and you will do so!

But don't think this is the end of your efforts. You still have to go a long way for greater victories, so be prepared for it. You will get great relief.

من نه آن رندم که ترک شاهد و ساغر کنم   محتسب داند که من این کارها کمتر کنم

من که عیب توبه کاران کرده باشم بارها   توبه از می وقت گل دیوانه باشم گر کنم

عشق دردانه‌ست و من غواص و دریا میکده   سر فرو بردم در آنجا تا بسر بردن کنم

لاله ساغرگیر و نرگس مست و بر ما نام فسق   داوری دارم بسی یا رب که را داور کنم

بازکش یکدم عنان ای ترک شهرآشوب من   تا ز اشک و چهره راهت پر زر و گوهر کنم

من که از یاقوت و لعل اشک دارم گنجها   کی نظر در فیض خورشید بلند اختر کنم

چون صبا مجموعه گل را به آب لطف شست   کج دلم خوان گر نظر بر صفحه دفتر کنم

عهد و پیمان فلک را نیست چندان اعتبار   عهد با پیمانه بندم شرط با ساغر کنم

من که دارم در گدایی گنج سلطانی به دست   کی طمع در گردش گردون دون پرور کنم

گر چه گردآلود فقرم شرم باد از همتم   گر آب چشمه خورشید دامن تر کنم

عاشقان را گر در آتش می‌پسندد لطف دوست   تنگ چشمم گر نظر در چشمه کوثر کنم

دوش لعلش عشوه‌ای می‌داد حافظ را ولی
من نه آنم کز وی این افسانه‌ها باور کنم

At dawn I tried for repentance an augury make,
Spring appeared putting repentance at stake.

I cannot suffer to see, I really think,
That I stand still and my rivals drink.

Smiling as bud, her party attend, O' boy,
Taking the cup I tore my cloak with joy.

Though a tavern beggar, yet when mellow,
I command the blue stars, my dear fellow.

Since I have not abstained from anything,
Why should blames on the libertines I bring?

On flower-throne my queen of beauties I place,
Of hyacinth and jasmine I make her a necklace.

Hafiz is fed up of secret drinking, so long,
He must drink now, hear lyre and sing a song.

INTERPRETATION

*It seems very hard for you to stand and watch things while your
rivals are enjoying success. You will also have a chance to enjoy such
pleasures; don't worry.*

With your lack of means you will still get a fair progress.

*The success you will gain, will make you much exalted and happy and
you will have a great celebration for it.*

بزم تو به سر گفتم استخاره کنم
بهار توبه شکن میرسد چه چاره کنم

سخن درست بگویم نمی توانم دید
که می خورند حریفان و من نظاره کنم

چو غنچه با لب خندان به یاد مجلس شاه
پیاله گیرم و از شوق جامه پاره کنم

بدور لاله دماغ مرا علاج کنید
گر از میانه بزم طرب کناره کنم

زروی دوست مرا چون گل مراد شکفت
حواله سر دشمن به سنگ خاره کنم

گدای میکده ام لیک وقت مستی بین
که ناز بر فلک و حکم بر ستاره کنم

مرا که نیست ره و رسم لقمه پرهیزی
چرا ملامت رند شرابخواره کنم

به تخت گل بنشانم بتی چو سلطانی
زسنبل و سمنش ساز طوق و یاره کنم

زبار خوردن پنهان ملول شد حافظ
بیا که بر بط و نی رازش آشکاره کنم

In flower season, wine I never forsake,
Claiming wisdom, never make such mistake.

Let the lyre players pleasant our time make.
My wisdom and piety I put at stake.

I'm fed up of school and its wrangle,
With wine and beauties myself will entangle.

Serve wine! This world fidelity never had.
Hearken tales of bygone kings— they're very sad.

My records are black; on resurrection day,
God's grace many such deeds will wash away.

Where is the morning breeze, so that I may,
Separation story to my friend convey?

Hafiz, this life is given you by the Friend,
Surrender—when you meet Him – in the end.

INTERPRETATION

When it is the time for joy, don't spend it otherwise. Perhaps you feel that you have too much time spent in the school and seminars. It may be wise to spend a little time in having some fun too. Don't take this life and its events very serious, for if you do, you will wake up at the end of your life to find out that your life has meant but worry and grief. Don't fear if certain things are not in your favor— God will certainly help you to fix them all up. You expect to go on a journey, when most of your difficulties will be solved. God bless you.

حاشا که من بہ بوسم گل ترک می کنم   من لاف عقل می زنم این کار کی کنم

مطرب کجاست تا همه محصول زهد و علم   در کار چنگ و بربط و آواز نی کنم

از قیل و قال مدرسه حالی دلم گرفت   یک چند نیز خدمت معشوق می کنم

کی بود در زمانه وفا جام می بیار   تا من حکایت جم و کاووس کی کنم

از نامهٔ سیاه نترسم که روز حشر   با فیض لطف او صد از این نامه طی کنم

کو پیک صبح تا گلهای شب فراق   با آن خجسته طالع فرخنده پی کنم

این جان عاریت که به حافظ سپرد دوست   روزی رخش ببینم و تسلیم وی کنم

I never forsake, my love, beauty and wine;
Repented hundred times, would do so no more.

Paradise and its beauties you may adore,
I give them all for the friend of mine.

Sometimes by a look many things you determine,
It isn't difficult to understand a metaphore.

Where is my heart? I can never score!
Until at the tavern, I taste my wine.

The admonitor said, "forget love, my friend",
"I won't do so, brother" I said, "don't fret".

I'm pious—like shamful Sheikhs I do not send ,
Love message to beauties on pulpit, I bet.

Hafiz, on Magi Sage you well depend,
Kiss his threshold, for, there,fortune you get.

INTERPRETATION

Few people in this world would be ready to sacrifice as much as you have done, in order to get what they desire. You have no rest until you get your heart's desire. Many people give you advice to give up your whole idea. But, you won't do so. The reason for your obstinacy is that you are sure of the good intention you have and of the wholesome means you have chosen. Your assurance is not in vain, for you will soon get great fortune as a result of your past efforts.

من ترک عشق شاهد و ساغر نمیکنم   صد بار توبه کردم و دیگر نمیکنم

باغ بهشت سایهٔ طوبی و قصر و حور   با خاک کوی دوست برابر نمیکنم

تلقین و درس اهل نظر یک اشارت است   گفتم کنایتی و مکرر نمیکنم

هرگز نمیشود ز سر خود خبر مرا   تا در میان میکده سر بر نمیکنم

ناصح به طعنه گفت که رو ترک عشق کن   محتاج جنگ نیست برادر نمیکنم

این تقویم تمام که با شاهدان شهر   ناز و کرشمه بر سر منبر نمیکنم

حافظ جناب پیر مغان جای دولت است   من ترک خاک بوسی این در نمیکنم

227

In the tavern I saw a light divine;
A strange light from strange place to shine!.

Haji! Don't be so proud and trust my word;
You see God's house only–I see the Lord;

I wish to get musk from my beauty's hair;
Of this impractical idea, I despair.

My sad heart, my night cry, my sigh and tear,
All in the hope of your grace I will bear.

Every moment new revelations I get.
I can't unfold what behind curtain I met.

No perfume nor musk you will ever see,
As her fragrance that Zephyr brought to me.

Friends! The love of Hafiz, do not object;
For him God's love is the only subject.

INTERPRETATION

You will receive relief and salvation from a place least expected. Many people have tried to do what you did, and have not derived the same successful results, because they have been very particular about outward appearances and formalities rather than realities and facts. Every day you will get new opportunities for your success. And the success you will gain will be unique in nature. The main reason for this is that your heart is truthful and you love God with a pure and unselfish aim.

در خرابات مغان نور خدا می‌بینم
این عجب بین که چه نوری ز کجا می‌بینم

جلوه بر من مفروش ای ملک الحاج که تو
خانه می‌بینی و من خانه خدا می‌بینم

خواهم از زلف بتان نافه گشایی کردن
فکر دور دست همانا که خطا می‌بینم

سوز دل اشک روان آه سحرگاه شب
این همه از نظر لطف شما می‌بینم

هر دم از روی تو نقشی زندم راه خیال
با که گویم که درین پرده چه‌ها می‌بینم

کس ندیدت که مشک ختن و نافه چین
آنچه من هر سحر از باد صبا می‌بینم

دوستان عیب نظر بازی حافظ مکنید
که من او را ز محبان شما می‌بینم

Blessed is the day when the ruined-home forsake,
With lifted soul, journey to my friend take,

A stranger may always go astray,
The scent of her hair is the guide of my way.

I feel depressed in Alexander's jail
I'll pack up—to Solomon's realm I'll sail.

Frail like Zephyr, but with impatient heart,
To my beautiful darling I will depart.

If for his love even my head I lose,
With sore heart and wet eyes this I'll choose.

I pledged to go to tavern happy and gay,
If I am relieved from worries some day.

Around Him like molecule I whirl in dance;
To Sun I ascend—to have of God a glance.

If like Hafiz, you ever became astray,
Light of his guidance you better obey.

INTERPRETATION

You expect to make a journey to some distant land. You are still at a dilemma as to whether this journey will be profitable for you or not. This journey will be by sea. You expect to meet a very good friend there. You do not mind the possible risks. This trip will bring you lots of honor and glory. God will lead you to safety and happiness all along your way.

230

خرم آن روز کزین منزل ویران بروم راحت جان طلبم وز پی جانان بروم

گرچه دانم که بجایی نبرد راه غریب من ببوی سر آن زلف پریشان بروم

دلم از وحشت زندان سکندر بگرفت رخت بربندم و تا ملک سلیمان بروم

چون صبا با تن بیمار و دل بی طاقت بهواداری آن سرو خرامان بروم

در رهِ او چو قلم گر به سرم باید رفت با دل زخم کش و دیده گریان بروم

نذر کردم گر از این غم به درآیم روزی تا درِ میکده شادان و غزل خوان بروم

بهواداری او ذره صفت رقص کنان تا لب چشمه خورشید درخشان بروم

تا زیان انجم احوال گرانباران نیست پارسایان مددی تا خوش و آسان بروم

و رچو حافظ ز بیابان نبرم ره بیرون
همره کوکبه آصف دوران بروم

We haven't come to this door for fame 'n' glory .
Resorted to it through   calamity and worry .

From naught we came to the mansion of love -
Such long journey we made from Heaven above.

We watched God's glory from the Paradise,
Came to share His glory—what a surprise !

In Heaven above there's a treasure so great,
Why then need help from king of a state ?

O' rescue ship! to anchor of grace move in ;
In God's sea of mercy we sink with sin .

O' sin-removing cloud pour out your rain !
Till eternity my record black'll remain.

Hafiz! Your woolly cloak away throw .
And this caravan follow with the sigh's glow .

INTERPRETATION

When you first accepted your career it was simply because of necessity. It has been a long and tedious course for you. But there will be good reward for all your work. You will get some unexpected benefit which will make your life rich and glorious. You will thus be relieved from the tedious work you have so far been doing.

ما بدین در نه پی حشمت و جاه آمده‌ایم / از بد حادثه اینجا به پناه آمده‌ایم

رهرو منزل عشقیم و ز سر حد عدم / تا به اقلیم وجود این همه راه آمده‌ایم

سبزه خط تو دیدیم و ز بستان بهشت / به طلب کاری این مهر گیاه آمده‌ایم

با چنین گنج که شد خازن او روح امین / بگدائی به در خانه شاه آمده‌ایم

لنگر حلم تو ای کشتی توفیق کجاست / که درین بحر کرم غرق گناه آمده‌ایم

آبرو می‌رود ای ابر خطا پوش ببار / که بدیوان عمل نامه سیاه آمده‌ایم

حافظ این خرقه پشمینه بینداز که ما / از پی قافله با آتش آه آمده‌ایم

As already stated, I repeat again,
It is not my choice if I'm led astray.

As parrot before mirror I try to say,
What Eternal Teacher bids me explain.

The rose and thorn'll go—Gardener'll remain,
As He wants us to grow we grow that way.

Friends! Forgive this heartless man, I pray;
Jewellers cost of my jewel ascertain.

Though red wine for dignified cloak is bad,
Never mind, my sham will wash away with wine.

Lovers some times may be happy or sad;
Joyful is night—sad is the dawn of mine .

Hafiz, won't smell tavern dust, my lad;
You'll smell dust as long as Sun'll shine.

INTERPRETATION

Sometimes you feel that you are not responsible for your past mistakes. You feel other people have pushed you into the things you did not like to do. Whatever your way of thinking may be, your greatest errors will bring you some light of relief and happiness, whereas, what you expect to bring you good results, will not do so.

234

بارها گفته‌ام و بار دگر می‌گویم   که من دلشده این ره نه بخود می‌پویم

در پس آینه طوطی صفتم داشته‌اند   آنچه استاد ازل گفت بگو می‌گویم

من اگر خارم و گر گل چمن آرایی هست   که از آن دست که او می‌کشدم می‌رویم

دوستان عیب من بیدل حیران مکنید   گوهری دارم و صاحب نظری می‌جویم

گر چه با دلق ملمع می گلگون عیب است   مکنم عیب کز و رنگ ریائی شویم

خنده و گریه عشاق ز جائی دگر است   می سرایم بشب و وقت سحری می‌مویم

حافظم گفت که خاک در میخانه مبوی

گو مکن عیب که من مشک ختن می‌بویم

Do you seek real wealth? It's to meet the friend.
To beg from God or a king? God I prefer.

It's not difficult the agony of death to suffer.
Friend's separation is hard to comprehend.

With tight heart as a bud, in garden I live;
Tearing off sham's cloak, chastity I pretend.

From the nightingale, love's secrets I portend.
Like breeze my love to my flower I give.

Before everything get from her lips a kiss,
Otherwise in the end this you will regret.

Cheer up! For when this byway you miss;
Another opportunity you will never get.

Hafiz has been deprived of the king's bliss,
O'Lord ! May the king never the Dervish forget.

INTERPRETATION

*You seek certain things that men will not easily give you, whereas
God will help you to get it all without men's help. You will be much
better appreciated and recognized by the people if you avoid any type
of sham or hypocrisy, and be exactly as your conscience bids you to
be. Before it may be too late, enjoy the blessings you already have at
your disposal.*

*As you expect, God will never forget you and will help you out
in your troubles.*

دانی که چیست دولت دیدار یار دیدن   در کوی او گدائی بر خسروی گزیدن

از جان طمع بریدن آسان بود ولیکن   از دوستان جانی مشکل توان بریدن

خواهم شدن بستان چون غنچه با دل تنگ   وانجا به نیک نامی پیراهنی دریدن

گه چون نسیم با گل راز نهفته گفتن   گه سر عشقبازی از بلبلان شنیدن

بوسیدن لب یار اول ز دست مگذار   کاخر ملول گردی از دست لب گزیدن

فرصت شمار صحبت کز این دو راهه منزل   چون بگذریم دیگر نتوان بهم رسیدن

گوئی برفت حافظ از یاد شاه یحیی   یارب بیادش آور درویش پروردن

I am known to make love throughout the town;
I can't see evil—won't pollute my gown.

I bear reproaches and am loyal and gay,
For in my creed it' s sin to be in dismay.

I asked the Sage: "What salvation brings up? "
"Forgive sinners" he said, lifting the cup

All who look at the world's garden of rose,
Desire to'pick your rose-beauty, I suppose.

I cast my lot on water, worshipping the drink;
Thus I destroy all, selfishness I think.

On the grace of your curls I rely. O'friend!
It's the only thing on which I can depend.

And now to the tavern I'll try to reach:
Fed up with those who don't do what they preach.

Learn a lesson from friend's charming beauty,
Who displaying beauty, considers it a duty.

Hafiz! Kiss the cup, and the Saki's chin;
To kiss hypocrites' hands is indeed a sin .

INTERPRETATION

*You are well known in your community for having a very high
taste, and all expect you to approach only the best. For this reason,
you are expected to do good to all who have done evil to you.The
majority of the people of your community have now the same object
and goal in mind as you have. They can give up their quest but you
will not do so. God's grace will come to you in time, for you have lost
hope in all human means.*

It is your imminent duty to be good and fair to other people.

منم که شهرهٔ شهرم به عشق ورزیدن   منم که دیده نیالوده‌ام به بد دیدن

وفا کنیم و ملامت کشیم و خوش باشیم   که در طریقت ما کافریست رنجیدن

به پیر میکده گفتم که چیست راه نجات   بخواست جام می و گفت عیب پوشیدن

مراد دل ز تماشای باغ عالم چیست   بدست مردم چشم از رخ تو گل چیدن

به می‌پرستی از آن نقش خود زدم بر آب   که تا خراب کنم نقش خود پرستیدن

به رحمت سر زلف تو واثقم ورنه   کشش چو نبود از آنسو چه سود کوشیدن

عنان به میکده خواهیم تافت زین مجلس   که وعظ بی عملان واجبست نشنیدن

ز خط یار بیاموز مهر با رخ خوب   که گرد عارض خوبان خوشست گردیدن

بموس جز لب ساقی و جام می حافظ   که دست زهد فروشان خطاست بوسیدن

239

Heaven's green-field and new Moon's scythe I saw;
I thought of seeds sown and the harvest I draw.

I said: "My luck slept and the Sun arose".
It said,"Don't be disappointed, I propose.

If you ascend as pure as Christ divine;
Your radiant rays the Sun will outshine.

The night-roving stars're unworthy of trust,
They reduced many famous kings to mere dust.

Gold and ruby ear- rings are dear in price-
Happy days will soon end, hearken my advice.

God protect her mole for in beauty's field,
The Sun and Moon to her challenge will yield.

O'Heaven, your grandeur does not display !
For Moon and pleiades are naught in love, I say.

Like tambourine, in this orbit keep your shape.
Don't go off your track, if slapped on the nape!

Hypocricy crop of faith will set afire -
Hafiz ! Your woolly cloak you don't require.

INTERPRETATION

As a result of your past toils, the fields are green and you have ripe opportunities before you. You get these benefits when you have been entirely disappointed. Yet you should be very careful about what will happen next, for the slightest mistake will bring great losses to you. Happy days will pass soon. But this does not mean that you will lose your benefits - on the contrary, they will remain with you for a relatively long time.

مزرع سبز فلک دیدم و داس مه نو / یادم از کشته خویش آمد و هنگام درو

گفتم ای بخت بخفتیدی و خورشید دمید / گفت با این همه از سابقه نومید مشو

گر روی پاک و مجرد چو مسیحا به فلک / از چراغ تو به خورشید رسد صد پرتو

تکیه بر اختر شب دزد مکن کاین عیار / تاج کاووس ببرد و کمر کیخسرو

گوشوار زر و لعل ار چه گران دارد گوش / دور خوبی گذران است نصیحت بشنو

چشم بد دور ز خال تو که در عرصه حسن / بیدقی راند که برد از مه و خورشید گرو

آسمان گو مفروش این عظمت کاندر عشق / خرمن مه به جوی خوشه پروین به دو جو

آتش زهد و ریا خرمن دین خواهد سوخت / حافظ این خرقه پشمینه بینداز و برو

از منت ای بره می باش و بفلا خفه گوش / که فضائی خوری ای ز دروازه خوش مرو

Why on lovers' separation you decide ?
Why you banish true lovers from your side ?

Give this thirsty desert tramp a drink;
You will do this for God's sake I should think .

You took my heart. I forgive, but warn thee;
Look after it better 'n you looked after me.

I can't bear to see, if you can suffer;
That my cup to other people you offer.

O' fly! High as falcon can never fly .
Lose prestige and bother us if you try.

It's your fault if you're deprived of God's door;
No use to worry— let us complain no more.

Hafiz ! Kings records of service require -
Unearned rights you have no right to aspire.

INTERPRETATION

You have decided to keep away from some of your best friends. This may bring about new difficulties for you. You also try to make the greatest possible progress, which is a little improportionate to your efforts and career. Do not have vain hopes—rather have practical aims and be sure you will make progress in proportion to your means.

You must bear in mind that rewards come in accordance with your efforts.

غزنیات حافظ

ای که مجوری مشتاق را امیدواری عاشقان را از بر خویش جدا میداری

تشنه با دیه راه هم بزلالی در یاب امیدی که درین ره بخدا میداری

دل ببردی وبجل کردست ای جانان به ازین وازنگاهش که مرا میداری

ساغر ماکه حریفان دگر می نوشند ماتحمل نکنیم ار تو روا میداری

ای مگس حضرت سیمرغ نه جولانگه تست عرض خودمی بری و زحمت ما میداری

تو بتقصیر خود افتادی ازین در محروم ازکه می نالی وفریاد چرا میداری

حافظ از پادشهان پایه بخدمت طلبند سعی نابرده چه امید عطا میداری

243

Try to be happy, now that there's Spring;
For when we die, many flowers the world 'll bring.

I don't say with whom to sit and what drink -
Your answers you know, if you wisely think .

The lyre tells same in metaphores I surmise;
Advice is effective, only if you're wise.

Every turf folio a living book I call,
A pity if you are ignorant of them all.

If you spend your time in worry and grief,
You waste your precious life in my belief.

Though the road to the friend is full of fears,
Yet if you know your way, easy it appears .

Hafiz, if luck is on your side, you may,
Be entrapped in her love-snare some day.

INTERPRETATION

*Happiness is something you can have in all circumstances of life—
but more so when the requisites for a happy life are all available.
You seem to possess most of these requisites, and so you must not
waste a minute of your life in melancholy thoughts. You are at liberty
to select your friends and associates, but always choose the best.*
*You may think that gaining success in your life is very difficult,
but if you know how to proceed it will be the easiest thing for you. In
your case you need a little good luck,- just a little good luck—to make
you get what you desire.*

244

نوبهار است در آن کوش که خوشدل باشی   که بسی گل بدمد باز و تو در گل باشی

من نگویم که کنون با که نشین و چه بنوش   که تو خود دانی اگر زیرک و عاقل باشی

چنگ در پرده همین می‌دهدت پند ولی   وعظت آنگه کند سود که قابل باشی

در چمن هر ورقی دفتر حالی دگر است   حیف باشد که ز کار همه غافل باشی

نقد عمرت ببرد غصه دنیا به گزاف   گر شب و روز در این قصه مشکل باشی

گر چه راهی‌ست پر از بیم ز ما تا بر دوست   رفتن آسان بود ار واقف منزل باشی

حافظا گر مدد از بخت بلندت باشد

صید آن شاهد مطبوع شمایل باشی

245

My love—like your beauty—perfect became.
Let's be happy; both are eternal, I proclaim .

If only one day of life with you I stay,
The happiest day of life will be that day.

When I'm with you a year seems a day.
A day without you is a year—I say .

O' beauty ! When in dream your face I grope;
Sleeping to my eyes is indeed vain hope.

Hafiz, if you seek her do not complain,
For long separation you still sustain.

INTERPRETATION

You seem to have reached the highest peak of happiness and per-fection in your life. Appreciate what you have and be careful how you dispense with these opportunities. Time passes only too quickly in these days of success, - so fast indeed that a year may look like a day. You are impatient to gain still more victories and successes. You will get them but it will take some time, as it needs the lapse of time in order to materialize.

بگرفت کار حُسنت چون مِهر خوبی بالی / خوش باش زانکه نبود این هر دو را زوالی

در وهم می‌نگنجد کاندر تصور عقل / آید به پیش معنی زین خوبی خجسته شمالی

شد حظ عمر حاصل گر زانکه با تو ما را / هرگز به مهر روزی روزی شود وصالی

آندم که با تو باشم یک سال هست روزی / وان دم که بی تو باشم یک لحظه هست سالی

چون من خیال رویت جانا بخواب بینم / کز خواب می نبیند چشم بجز خیالی

رحم آر بر دل من کز مهر روی خوبت / شد شخص ناتوانم باریک چون هلالی

حافظ مکن شکایت گر وصل دوست خواهی / زین بیشتر بباید بر هجرت احتمالی

A message from a mendicant to a king you tell: -
"Kingdoms at tavern for a cup' ll sell."

Libertine and scoundrel though I truly became,
By grace of the friend I will get good name.

You who possess elixir! Pity my despair,
I have no gold to give - so lay a snare.

The friend paid me no attention at any stage;
No answer to love-letter or message.

My wine is crude; let the Sheikh enjoy fame;
Drink crude wine— hypocricy don't proclaim .

O' Sheikh your rosaries don't cheat me, beware !
Tricks do not put clever birds in snare.

To whom, of my worries should I complain ?
Your lips give life—but won't long remain .

The darts of her lashes Hafiz can't miss;
He can't revenge on a murderer like this.

INTERPRETATION

Wake up ! If you have a pure heart and clear vision, you will not pay any attention to kingdoms—they will have no charm for you! It is true that you have overstepped a little the limits of your possibilities, and expect bad results for it, but rest assured that God will help you out and will relieve you from your troubles. The outcome will be to your benefit and good name.

You will find that many of your efforts will bring you no immediate results. Many of your requests will also not be attended to or replied. But you will finally receive help and relief, though this relief will not remain long with you. You must be prepared for further battles and campaigns.

که بر و بنه و شاهان ز من گدا پیامی   کبکوی می فروشان و هزار جم بجامی

شده‌ام خراب بدنام و هنوز امیدوارم   که جهت عزیزان برسم به نیک نامی

تو که کیمیا فروشی نظری بقلب ما کن   که بضاعتی نداریم و فکنده‌ایم دامی

عجب از وفای جانان که عنایتی نفرمود   نه بنامه نه پیامی نه بخانه نه سلامی

اگر این شراب خامست اگر آن حریف پخته   بهزار بار بهتر ز هزار پخته خامی

ز رهم میفکن ای شیخ بدانهای تسبیح   که چو مرغ زیرک افتد نفتد بهیچ دامی

سر خدمت تو دارم بخرم بلطف و مفروش   که چو بنده کمتر افتد ببها رکی غلامی

کجا برم شکایت بکه گویم این حکایت   که لبت حیات ما بود و نداشتی دوامی

بگشای تیر مژگان و بریز خون حافظ

که چنان کشنده‌ای را نکند کس انتقامی

I love you and sure you know it, my soul !
Don't read or look—you comprehend the whole .

Between two lovers quarrels there may be,
But blind enemies love secrets cannot see.

Angel adored Adam after HIS image;
But saw HIS beauty surpassed man's stage.

The scent of your curls to my eyes brings life,
O'Lord, never give me separation-strife .

Pleasures of night in the dawn-sleep disappear
You appreciate time when it's gone I fear.

Of human brothers don't be annoyed, my boy .
Suffer present hardships for future joy.

Hafiz! the thought of her locks led you astray,
Never try the impossible luck, I pray .

INTERPRETATION

You may have disagreements with your collaborators, but these disagreements won't be serious, though people around you may often think it will be so. The thought of success in your plans gives you new life and strength, and this will make you succeed. But happiness, as sorrow, will soon end, and you will wake up to see that your dreams of success are over. Nevertheless, don't give up your campaign, but work hard and be sure the future is bright for you, bringing you many fruitful results. You will succeed but within the limits of reason.

که هم نادیده می بینی و هم نوشته میخوانی

هواخواه توام جانا و میدانم که میدانی

نبیند چشم بینا خصوص اسرار پنهانی

ملامت گو چه دریا بد میان عاشق و معشوق

که از هر رقعه و نقش هزاران به پریشانی

بنشان لف صوفی را بپا بازی و قصه آور

خدا را یک نفس بنشین گره بگشا ز پیشانی

مشاد کار مستمندان در آن ابروی دلبند

که در حسن تو لطفی و بدبیش از حد انسانی

ملک در سجده آدم زمین بوس تو نیت کرد

مبادا این جمع را یا رب غم از باد پریشانی

چراغ افروز چشم ما نسیم زلف جانانست

ندانی قدر وقت ای دل گر آن وقتی که در مانی

در نفا عیش شبگیری که در خواب سحر گذشت

کبش دشواری منزل بپا و عهد آسانی

ملول از همرهان بودن طریق کاردانی نیست

خیال چنبر زلفش فریب ت میدهد حافظ

که تا حلقه اقبال ممکن نجنبانی

Relieve yourself from sorrows—hear my advice.
Give up the impossible; with blood you pay the price.

Like clay you're shaped by the potter's skill,
Your jug with wine you better try to fill.

If you intend paradise beauties to get,
The earthly beauties then you must forget.

In vain you can't yourself a great man call,
Unless the means of greatness you have all.

Queen of Beauties! You will receive rewards!
If for lonesome Hafiz you have kind regards.

Hafiz, if you entrust your Fate to grace,
Lots of good fortune you will soon embrace.

INTERPRETATION

Your ambitions must be practical ones, and not utopia. If you seek certain blessings, you must be prepared to dispense with other blessings. If you seek a great name, you must create in yourself and around you all the means and qualifications of greatness. In other words, everything requires adequate means, without which one fails to achieve. You must get your means and be prepared for your campaign. When you do that, be sure the results will be very outstanding and will bring you lots of success and opportunities.
So, do your best and leave to God the rest.

بشنو این نکته که خود را ز غم آزاده کنی   خون خوری گر طلب روزی ننهاده کنی

آخر الاامر گل کوزه گران خواهی شد   حالیا فکر سبو کن که پر از باده کنی

گر از آن آدمیانی که بهشتت هوس است   عیش با آدمیی چند پری زاده کنی

تکیه بر جای بزرگان نتوان زد به گزاف   مگر اسباب بزرگی همه آماده کنی

اجرها باشدت ای خسرو شیرین دهنان   گر نگاهی سوی فرهاد دل افتاده کنی

خاطرت کی رقم فیض پذیرد هیهات   مگر از نقش پراکنده ورق ساده کنی

کار خود گر به کرم بازگذاری حافظ   ای بسا عیش که با بخت خداداده کنی

ای صبا بندگی خواجه جلال الدین کن

که جهان پر سمن و سوسن آزاده کنی

253

Saki! Watch the cloud's shade, the brook, the Spring!
You know my heart's desire–then wine bring.

No truth from Sufi's shamful cloak you gain;
Rise and with pure wine wash out your stain.

Thank God the Spring has come again indeed,
Search for truth and plant seeds of good deed.

If you seek friend, clean the mirror of your heart,
Or else a piece of glass no beauty' ll impart.

"Open your ears!" Nightingale cries in distress;
Never find fault, if you seek success.

You said, "Hafiz, will also sham display",
Thanks to your judgement! Is that fair to sav?

INTERPRETATION

There are times when all means of joy and fun are available, and if you fail to use them, you have lost golden chances. You will soon find that the best way to get what you want is to go straight to it, and do not hide your intentions, for this straigtforward attitude will help you to succeed. Truth and honesty are your best means of support. Stick to them and you will have what you seek. Of course, a pure heart, requires you to do good, and to close your ears and mouth to harmful talks about other people. If you do these, you will succeed in your life.

ساقیا سایه ابرست و بهار و لب جوی / من نگویم چه کن ای اهل دلی خود تو بگوی

بوی یکرنگی ازین نقش نمی آید خیز / دلق آلوده و صوفی بی ناب بشوی

سفله طبعت جهان بر کرمش تکیه مکن / ای جهان دیده ثبات قدم ازسفله مجوی

و نصیحت کنمت بشنو و صد گنج ببه / از در عیش درآ و بره عیب مپوی

شکر آنرا که دگر بازرسیدی بهار / بیخ نیکی بنشان و ره تحقیق بجوی

روی جانان طلبی آینه را قابل ساز / ورنه هرگز گل و نسرین ندمد زآهن و روی

گوش کن پند ای که ببل نغنان بیگوید / خواجه تقصیر مفرما ما کل توفیق بجوی

گفتی از حافظ ما بوی ریا می آید / آفرین بر نفست باد که خوش بردی بوی

The nightingale on cypress branch remained,
Last night in high tunes many truths explained :-

"Come, Moses fire appeared on the bush today,
"Secrets of divine unity, bushes display.

"The witty birds in the garden will appear,
"Enjoy drink, while their love-songs you hear.

"Of Jam's cup you hear, though Jam made no gain,
"The world's riches won't forever remain.

"Listen my story, so strange and yet so sad,
"My friend killed me though Christ's breath he had."

Many hearts are mad because of your wink,
With your languishing eyes no need for drink.

How well the farmer advised his offspring,
"Seeds sown today, tomorrow fruits bring."

Saki served Hafiz with excessive drink,
His turban and cloak are all disturbed, I think.

INTERPRETATION

Every thing seems ripe for your triumph now. Take full advantage of all your means and make the great success you expect to make. Remember that conditions change quickly and so you must take full advantage of all your available resources and possibilities.

You expect a great privilege from a well-known source, but this may not come to you yet. You will certainly reap the fruits of all your deeds. Expect a brilliant tomorrow, for you are not failing in your efforts, and, do your best.

بلبل ز شاخ سرو به گلبانگ پهلوی — می‌خواند دوش درس مقامات معنوی

یعنی بیا که آتش موسی نمود گل — تا از درخت نکته توحید بشنوی

مرغان باغ قافیه سنجند و بذله‌گو — تا خواجه می خورد به غزل‌های پهلوی

جمشید جز حکایت جام از جهان نبرد — زنهار دل مبند بر اسباب دنیوی

این قصه عجب شنو از بخت واژگون — ما را بکشت یار به انفاس عیسوی

خوش وقت بوریا و گدایی و خواب امن — کاین عیش نیست درخور اورنگ خسروی

چشمت به غمزه خانه مردم خراب کرد — مخموریت مبادا که خوش‌ست می‌روی

وهمتان ساخوره چه خوش گفت پیر ما — کای نور چشم من به جز از کشته ندروی

ساقی بیار لطیفه حافظ زیاده گو
کاشفته گشت طره دستار مولوی

بنیاد هستی تو چو زیر و زبر شود — در دل مدار هیچ که زیر و زبر شوی

گر در سرت هوای وصال‌ست حافظا — باید که خاک درگه اهل هنر شوی

O'ignorant, try in wisdom to abide!
Be a disciple before you are a guide.

In school of love your teacher you obey.
Become mature in love-secrets some day.

Like men of truth, all existence forget.
Love-elixir changes you to gold, I bet.

If you eat and sleep, your status 'll degrade.
Forget the flesh and a saint you 'll be made.

In your mortal heart there is love divine.
With that, the firmament Sun you 'll outshine.

If you dive in divine sea don't fret;
For even the seven seas won't make your hair wet.

Emerge in God's true love from head to feet,
And the God of love you'll certainly meet.

If God's satisfaction is your main aim,
In spiritual insight you get good fame.

If all existence is bound to destroy,
If you abide in love you 'll live in joy.

Hafiz! If the grace of friend expect,
Dust of men of insight you should respect.

INTERPRETATION

Perhaps you want to climb to the highest peak of ambition or education without having the patience to climb step by step—to be a disciple first before you become a teacher or leader. This will lead you to a very dependable and bright future, which will be envied by many. There will be dangers on your way, but God will save you from all of them. There may be troubles for many around you , but with your pure heart you are sure to survive and live successfully.

ای بی‌خبر بکوش که صاحب‌خبر شوی   تا راهرو نباشی کی راهبر شوی

در مکتب حقایق پیش ادیب عشق   هان ای پسر بکوش که روزی پدر شوی

دست از مس وجود چو مردان ره بشوی   تا کیمیای عشق بیابی و زر شوی

خواب و خورت ز مرتبه خویش دور کرد   آنگه رسی به خویش که بی خواب و خور شوی

گر نور عشق حق به دل و جانت اوفتد   بالله کز آفتاب فلک خوبتر شوی

یک دم غریق بحر خدا شو گمان مبر   کز آب هفت بحر به یک موی تر شوی

از پای تا سرت همه نور خدا شود   در راه ذوالجلال چو بی پا و سر شوی

وجه خدا اگر شودت منظر نظر   زین پس شکی نماند که صاحب نظر شوی

Like Jam take the cup— great secrets it displays,
Two-world 's secrets unfold its radiant rays.

At the tavern-door vagrant libe. rines stay,
Crowns of kings they take but freely give away.

Brick 's my pillow, my feet on seven seas rest
Note my mighty honor 'n' situation abreast.

Watch the tavern, though its walls not high,
They reach firmament high up in the sky.

Don't spend life without guide to your way,
Dark road you have to pass— don't go astray.

O' Heart, if kingdom of contentment you get;
You take from the Moon to the fish, I bet.

All men can't be poor and riches forsake-
Very few indeed prefer poverty to take.

Hafiz! Of vain hopes you must be ashamed;
With black records how paradise you aimed?!

INTERPRETATION

You may not be very rich, but money seems not so important to you. You get money and spend it like children use gravel. Nevertheless, you are going to have a great chance of having lots of wealth and money. Meantime, if you have some good guides or counsellors, you will do much better. You will have to pass through dark roads, and, to do this successfully, you must benefit from the experience of well-informed men. With some self-sufficiency and contentment, you are apt to climb very high up.

سحرم هاتف میخانه به دولتخواهی   گفت باز آی که دیرینه این درگاهی

همچو جم جرعه ما کش که ز سرّ دو جهان   پرتو جام جهان بین به تو آگه سازد

بر در میکده و زندان قلندر بنشینند   که تسانند و دهند افسر شاهی به ثنا

خشت زیر سر و بر تارک هفت اختر پای   دست قدرت نگر و منصب صاحب جاهی

سر ما و در میخانه که طرف بامش   بفلک بر شده و دیوار بدین کوتاهی

قطع این مرحله بی همرهی خضر مکن   ظلمات است بترس از خطر گمراهی

اگرت سلطنت فقر ببخشند ای دل   کمترین ملک تو از ماه بود تا ماهی

تو دم فقر ندانی ز خود این دست مده   مسند خواجگی و مجلس توران شاهی

حافظ خام طمع شرمی از این قصه بدار
علت چیست که فردوس برین نخواهی

A greeting warm—as fragrance of the friend—
To that Light-of-the-World, sincerely send.

Cordial greeting from a devoted heart,
To that intimate friend, I truly impart.

Alas! All my good friends have passed away.
My heart aches, Saki! Where you stay?

From the Magi's altar, never turn your face,
Keys to all secrets are sold in that place.

My sweetheart, though with a beauty sublime,
Is inclined to disloyalty to me,sometime.

My soul never had high aims in its quest;
Yet from the hard-hearted I make no request.

Where intoxicating wine they sell, you say?
Perhaps from shamful Sheikh I may break away.

My friends broke their covenants, I am so sad;
They acted as if no acquaintance we had.

O selfishness! Leave me, you greedy thing;
Though a mendicant, I will live like a king.

This is elixir of happiness, I say :
"Keep away from all bad company—keep away!"

Hafiz! Of world's injustice don't complain,
None of God's creatures eternal remain.

INTERPRETATION

You will soon send a cordial message to one of the great men of your country. This will lead to a brighter and better future. You will soon be dealing with very important affairs. But the chances are that you will have variable situations all the time. You will find that many of your friends will forsake you. But working all alone, you will be able to push your way through successfully.

بدان مردم دیده روشنائی
سلامی چو بوی خوش آشنائی

بدان شمع خلوتگه پارسائی
درودی چو نور دل پارسایان

دلم خون شد از غصه ساقی کجائی
نمی بینم از همدمان هیچ بر جای

فروشند مفتاح مشکل گشائی
ز کوی مغان رخ مگردان کانجا

زهد مپر و شیوهٔ بیوفائی
عروس جهان گرچه در حد حسن است

نخواهد ز رنگین دلان کیمیائی
دل خستهٔ من گرش همتی هست

که در تابم از دست بی سر و پائی
می صوفی افکن کجا می فروشند

که گوئی نبود دوست خود آشنائی
رفیقان چنان عهد صحبت شکستند

بسی پادشائی کنم در گدائی
مرا گر تو بگذاری ای نفس طامع

ز همصحبت بد جدائی جدائی
بیاموزت کیمیای سعادت

مکن حافظ از جور دوران شکایت

چه دانی تو ای بنده کار خدائی

263

O Queen of Beauties! How lonely I live!
Come and with your presence my heart relieve.

The flowers will not always bring romance;
Help poor people, now that you have the chance.

I complained to Zephyr of the friend's tress;
"Forget complaints", it said, "She'll redress .

"Hundred Zephyrs are dancing under her chain,
"Tell your heart vague hopes never entertain."

The fact that I love you and you're away,
Took all patience, leaving me in dismay.

O'Lord, to whom this truth I shall reveal?
Though present everywhere, yourself conceal!

Saki! Rose is attractive for your sake.
Your cypress the garden attractive'll make.

When disappointed, your love is my cure.
In your good memory hardships I endure.

In the circle of Fate, as a spot I surrender,
What God desires is good,this I remember!

Libertinism requires self-sacrifice indeed—
Self-conceit is profanity in my creed.

Hafiz! Separation ends–You'll see the friend.
Good news for you! Disappointments will soon end.

INTERPRETATION

*You expect a good friend to come from a journey and to brighten
your society. He or she will come soon and will be a better friend for
you after his or her return. But never expect to have her or him exclu -
sively; for other people have also interests in him or her.*

*Your separation from the friend will soon end, and so will all
your disappointments.*